DIALOGUE WITH SINGLE PARENTS

PASTOR JEFFREY A. JOHNSON, SR.

xulon
PRESS

To Mary Coleman, my beloved mother,
who approached becoming a single parent in the same way she
approached every circumstance in life—
with a deep love for God,
a strong faith that would not give up,
and an extraordinary love for her children
that prompted her to give all that she had day after day
to see our needs met and God's will accomplished in our lives.

Although God eventually brought a wonderful man into her life,
and ours,
I do not forget the years that she led her young family alone—
teaching us to love God, respect others, and value ourselves.

Proverbs 31:26-28 says of the honorable woman:
She speaks with wisdom,
and faithful instruction is on her tongue.
She watches over the affairs of her household
and does not eat the bread of idleness.
Her children arise and call her blessed.

Today, along with my sister and brothers,
I rise up and call our mother blessed . . . and much, much loved.

TABLE OF CONTENTS

DIALOGUE WITH MY MOTHER

There is only one single parent whom I have had the opportunity to observe up close and personal over a period of years. That parent is Mary Coleman, my mother. I didn't get *glimpses* of her dealings with her children; I experienced them personally every day. From the love and joy that is still in our family now that all four of us children are grown, I know that what she did worked. While writing this book, I sat down with my mother to ask her some questions about *how* she made it work. I believe that the responses drawn from our conversation will be a benefit and blessing to other single parents, so I offer you now as the Foreword...

Dialogue with My Mother

This book is a dialogue with single parents. I am trying to help single parents know how to deal with circumstances they face in life. In most cases, this is not a situation they have chosen and it is one that challenges them day after day. Mother, you not only survived being a single parent; but you thrived. In order to offer your experience as a way to inspire and encourage other single parents, I am going to ask you several questions that I believe get to the heart of some of the issues that confront them.

So, you were married, had four children, and things fell apart. Your husband left and you had to deal with these children by yourself. How did you feel about suddenly finding yourself in that situation?

> *I'll be honest with you, Son. I was shouting with joy when he was gone. Our marriage wasn't working. He wasn't working. His role in the home wasn't working. I was a young mother trying to care for four children, and I was doing it alone. His body was there, but his commitment to our marriage and our family left long before his body walked out the door. When he left, it meant that I had one less mouth to feed, one less person for whom I was responsible. Caring for children is one thing, but caring for a grown man who is acting like a child is something else entirely. The only thing that made me feel sorry when your daddy left was that all of you children were sad. But I had protected you so that you did not see your daddy as I saw him, and you were too young to understand.*

When he left, how did you start dealing with your new reality?

> *I kept my job. After he left, I consciously decided, "Okay, I can deal with this." I always had a good job. I became a nurse when I was twenty. I could always put food on the table and a roof over our heads. I had no problem with that. I didn't get any support from him. We didn't live in luxury, but we did okay on our own.*

I didn't even know we didn't have much until I went to college. I thought everybody lived like we did. In contrast, *my* son Jay didn't know we had anything until he went to college and found out not everybody lives like we do. What you did for our family served as a foundation that allowed *me* to do even more for *my* family. Was there anything you learned from Grandmother or Granddaddy that helped you with your children?

It's a different age now, but I learned to respect older people. We used to respect our neighbors and do for them like we were doing for our own. I hope that I instilled the value of community in my children, and the sense of respect and caring for others.

What kind of help did you get from others after you were left to support four children alone? To whom did you turn for support?

My family was there. They supported me. We were a close family. They encouraged me. When I went to work, my mother kept you. Dad took care of you all. He was the overseer. My sisters also lived in the same neighborhood. I had to work. I was trying to put food on the table and coats on your backs in the winter. Someone had to bring in the bread. But my family helped me. Because of all of them, we didn't have any major problems from day to day. Or, if we did, you all didn't tell me about them.

We also had some great neighbors who stepped in to provide support in different ways. One family we were especially close to had children about the same ages as some of you. Wesley Gordon was their father. You'll remember that his son was your best friend. Mr. Gordon reached out to you even as if you were his own child. You and his son both went out for football, but I couldn't afford to buy your uniform. Mr. Gordon bought your uniform for you and wouldn't let me even try to help out a little with the cost. When he took his son to football practice, he took you as well. When he took his son to a football game, he took you with them, too. I don't know what we would have done had he not been there for you at that particular time. I think God had him there because He knew that you needed father figures, and I think he made a real difference in your life.

What about the church? You kept taking us to church all the time. The church must have been part of your support system.

> *Oh, yes. Rev. Charles Harris let you know who Jesus is. And Sister Dorothy Richards taught you. Do you remember Sister Richards? She loved you, Jeffrey.*

She still comes to church. She was at church last Sunday. And how did you feel about God at this time. Did you ever become angry with God or blame God for your circumstances?

> *Oh, no. You don't get mad at God. I was never upset with God. I knew that nothing that happened was God's fault. We were just two young people who got married too soon. But when your daddy walked out, God stayed with us.*

You said earlier that you were a nurse at age twenty. You had four children by the time you were twenty-two. That means you became a nurse before I was born—when you were pregnant with Tonette and Tony. You were working and going to school while you had one child and were pregnant with twins. Today, we have so many teenagers having kids. And they say they can't go to school because they have so much going on. But you had a child and a husband; you were pregnant with twins: and still you worked *and* went to school. How did you do that?

> *Carefully. You can do it, but you just have to stay focused. You can't do everything else—like going nightclubbing and whatever else the other young folks were doing. I didn't do any of that because I didn't have time. I had learned that we have to make choices in life; we can't have it all. Being the oldest of nine children made me mature early. Even as a child, I thought things out before I acted. So, thinking through how we were going to care for our growing children, I decided I needed to get an LPN license so*

that I would have more coming in than just a min-imum wage.

You make it sound so simple: "I just went on to school." But it couldn't have been like that. You had to find time to study. You had to go to classes. You had to go to the library, get your work done on time, and still take care of a family. It had to be hard work. What kept you motivated?

> *I don't remember it being hard. I was determined. When you have that determination, it energizes you. I started off working in a kitchen. Then one day, I went up to where the nurses were working and I said, "I can do that." So I went to school then and became a licensed practical nurse. I was twenty when I was an LPN. After handling the responsibility and the workload at work at that level, I decided to go back and become a registered nurse. When I got my RN, I could do some things I'd never done before. That's when we started to live a little bit better, because I was earning a little more money.*

When you were working on your nursing degree, that was over fifty years ago. That was the time of open racism. People put African Americans down because of the color of our skin. They didn't give us opportunities. How did you live above that? Some people experience that and say, "I can't make it because I'm a Black female and the White majority looks down on Black women." But you didn't do that. You were still able to achieve. How did you rise above racism, the Jim Crow laws, having to go to the back door of public places, and all of that? How did you succeed at a time when people would tell you that you couldn't do it?

> *They didn't tell me that. No, they encouraged me. Because I was such a good worker and I got along with all people, they wanted me to succeed. I had the kind of personality that they wanted me to do it.*

Even though you had a better job, you still had only one income in the family, and four children needing food, clothes, transportation, medical and dental work, money for things at school, and the list goes on and on. How did you manage your money?

> *I know you won't like my answer, but in all honesty, Jeffrey, I didn't actually <u>manage</u> money. I always had a good job. And since I had a decent income, I just paid my bills. My mother used to tell me, "You just spend money and spend money." I did. I never did manage money. But the one thing I did do was to keep my priorities straight. I always made sure I paid bills before buying something extra just because one of us wanted it. That's why we didn't have all the things we wanted, but we did have everything we needed.*

Black people now are doing some things they didn't do generally fifty years ago. That may be true of other groups as well, but I know it is true of us. Black people didn't used to commit suicide, but now we attempt that at a high rate. It's really sad. Some single parents might think, "I've got four children to raise. I have to do everything alone. I can't handle this," and decide to commit suicide. How did you keep from doing that?

> *It wasn't on the list of things to do. That thought didn't even come up. I always had a will to live.*

Walking away from the family is another way out. How did you keep from leaving us?

> *I loved you all. I didn't want to leave you. You were my responsibility.*

You had four children—three of whom were boys. I know some of the crazy things I did. I won't tell on my brothers and sister, but I know some of the crazy things they did, too. Yet we all turned out okay. What were your thoughts about discipline?

If there was anything I wish I had done differently in terms of parenting, it is in the area of discipline. But I raised all of you just as my parents had raised us. In those days, if you didn't act right, they whipped your butt. They didn't sit you in a corner for five minutes. So, when you did something wrong, I beat your butt instead of giving you all a time out. I'm thankful for the way you all turned out, but I think that I could have been less harsh and you still would have turned out well. It isn't that I see anything wrong with a spanking when it is appropriate, but there are other effective methods of discipline and I wish I had known about them.

You were divorced when I was eight. You were young and beautiful and men were attracted to you. But you didn't remarry until I was thirteen or fourteen. Why did you wait so long to marry again?

I didn't want to get married again. I didn't want to bring anybody in on my kids. I had boyfriends, but I never let them come around my kids. I wasn't going to bring a man into your lives until I knew he was ready to say, "I do." He could meet my kids after he asked, "Will you marry me?" I wasn't perfect, but I didn't bring ugliness around you all. I wasn't going to get you caught up in the trauma and drama of relationships. I wasn't going to have you wondering, "Is this my new daddy?" And I waited until you all got old enough so that you could tell me if somebody did something to you. If anybody had done anything to my kids, God would have had to intervene to keep me out of prison. No, I didn't bring anybody around you all.

No you didn't. Not till Alonzo Coleman came into the picture and started bringing us pizza. What made you choose Alonzo out of all of the men who were trying to take you out?

He treated me special. He opened doors for me, spoke kindly to me, and watched out for me—even in little ways, like making sure my seatbelt was on. But I liked that he was kind to everybody. He wasn't just doing something for me to impress me, so I knew that he wouldn't be changing up on me when we got married. I didn't think that I was anything special, but he made me feel special. He took me to nice places, nice restaurants. He saw things in me, good things that I didn't see in myself. And he loved my children. He knew that I came as a package deal and he embraced all of us.

We got married in Mississippi. He took me down there to meet his family. He loved his family and wanted them to like me and to be happy for us. Once that was assured, he was ready to get married. I didn't even know what he had in mind until he said, "Let's go over to the courthouse and do it now." I was ready, so we did it. We had a happy marriage. He was a good guy to me. I've had a good life, a wonderful life, an excellent life.

Before Alonzo came along, where were you with God? You were probably thirty years old when my father left. You were raising four children by yourself. How was your prayer life back then? It's probably hard to see while you're going through it. But as you look back over it, how do you see God in all of that? You were going to school, getting your nursing degree, caring for four children, paying bills— how did you see God in the midst of that chaos?

I was always okay with God. I had a blessed life, and I knew that God was the basis for it. I was a Sunday school teacher, so I was always studying and reading. You have to teach yourself before you can teach someone else, so I learned a lot. That helped me deal with my circumstances. It kept me grounded.

> *I think you see life differently when you are looking*
> *from God's perspective. You recognize that God has*
> *a purpose for your life. You just stay in your purpose.*
> *In life, you go through different phases, different pur-*
> *poses. At that time, my purpose was raising my kids.*

Did you actually believe the stuff you read in the Bible? Every now and then, I memorize certain scriptures—just for myself, not for any other reason. Were there any scriptures that you clung to and held on to when things got difficult?

> *Yes, I believed what I read in the Bible. I still do. I*
> *don't recall specific verses that I clung to at that time,*
> *but the Bible keeps you anchored. It keeps you from*
> *getting discouraged.*

I'm going to take this to a personal level now. When you see me preaching and you hear people talk about the impact my ministry has had on their lives, what do you think? What's going through your head?

> *God is doing it. I always think that because God's*
> *anointing is on you.*

Because I'm a pastor, some people seem to think I was raised in heaven and then came down here as a fully grown man of God. (They have no idea that I had to come *up* to where I am today.) Did you ever think you were raising a preacher? Did you recognize that there was an anointing on my life and start preparing me for the ministry?

> *No! That wasn't my job. That was God's job. He did*
> *a great job. I remember when you were seventeen*
> *and you came in to talk to me. I think I was in bed at*
> *the time. You told me you were called to preach, and*
> *I asked, "Who called you?" You said, "God." After*
> *saying that, you walked out of the room. I was glad*

you did because I wouldn't have known what to say at that time. I was trying to focus. I was wondering, "Is he kidding or what?"

You see, I was still looking at what you had been in the past, not what God was going to make of you in the future. You were my baby, the baby of the family. And, in fact, when you were little, you were a cry baby. We used to count how many times a day you would cry. I'm serious. It got up to seventeen times a day. I counted them because it became embarrassing. So, while I loved you and I was proud of you, I could not have imagined all that God had in store for you. In fact, I had never before personally seen God do such miraculous things in anybody's life. So there is no way I could have anticipated where God has taken you—I didn't know such a place existed.

Now that we're all grown, have families, have given you grandchildren, and are doing well, what do you think now? Do you ever think, "None of this would be happening if it weren't for me"?

No, I think, "It's amazing. It really is. It's just amazing." We had a good life. You all didn't miss a meal. You had clothes on and a roof over your head. And now I have a good family. Now that I am elderly, I have a daughter who takes such good care of me that she meets my needs before I know I have a need; and I have three sons who are each so special to me in their own way. I wouldn't trade my family or my life for anything.

We know that there will be a young single parent reading this book one day who is tempted to give up. Whatever the situation, this person is raising children alone. What one last word do you have for single parents? When they are ready to give up and let someone else take over, what would you tell them?

No one can take care of your kids like you can.

Was it was worth hanging in there? Are you glad you stayed?

Yes!

I love you, Mother.

Introduction:

This Book Is for Everybody

As I am writing this book, *Dialogue with Single Parents*, I am aware that I am writing not *only* to single parents. Most of us are related to a single parent in one way or another and we can develop a greater understanding for what that person is experiencing in his or her position. Some who read this book will gain greater insight into the family in which they grew up, which was headed by a single parent. Some who are parents will pick up pointers along the way that will make them better parents. And some who are not parents, and perhaps not even married, will recognize spiritual principles that are applicable to many facets of their lives. So this book is for *everybody*.

A child living in America in the twenty-first century is more likely to grow up in a household with one parent than a two-parent household. Sixty percent of babies born in the United States are born to single parents. Eighty percent of babies born to Blacks in the U.S. are born to single parents. With 40 to 50 percent of first marriages and even higher percentages of second and third marriages ending in divorce, there are many single-parent homes in America.

God has put this group of people on my heart and has led me to address their unique set of needs and challenges. As a father of four sons, I know how difficult parenting is even with two loving, caring parents in the home. When I think about single parents trying to do all of this alone, my heart goes out to them, along with my deepest admiration and respect.

I spent part of my childhood in a single-parent home. I saw first-hand what my own mother went through, and I know what I experienced personally. In a sense, this book is not only written from the perspective of a pastor wanting to share advice and inspiration from the Word of God. This book is also written from the heart of that little boy I once was, the little boy who saw his daddy leave and never come back. I can look back now and make meaning of some things that I could not see while I was young and in the midst of those circumstances. I can reflect now upon my situation and my mother's with the vantage point of years of watching God work, even in the midst of our circumstances, to care for us and give us lives filled with love, joy, and purpose.

In this book I speak to single parents directly, but with the understanding that others will be reading the book also, and this book is for them as well. All of us are influenced by single parents in one way or another because we are related through our families, neighborhoods, churches, and communities. And we all influence those single parents by our words and our behavior towards them.

We need to get beyond our misunderstandings regarding single parents. We often miss the mark because we get caught up in myths and misinformation. Instead, I want us to create a culture in our churches, communities, and families that doesn't condemn single parents, but comforts them; that doesn't judge them, but brings joy to them; that doesn't put them down, but lifts them up. To establish this kind of culture, we have to get beyond the myths.

One of the myths that must be discarded involves the notion that most single parents are teenage girls who have borne three and four children before they get married. Yet that is not the case. Most single parents are forty years old, and a majority of them have only one child.

Another of the myths is that single parents are girls who got caught up in a series of illicit sexual activity. That is not the case. Most single parents started off in committed, loving, healthy relationships, but the relationships went awry and no longer worked. Some people are also single parents by choice. They took in someone else's child. They became a guardian or adopted a child out of love for that child and a desire to help that child succeed in life. Some grandparents chose to raise their grandchildren because their son or daughter could not or would not be a good parent to those little ones. Some single parents are widows or widowers. We've got to get beyond the myths.

A third myth is that all single parents are irresponsibly having children and expecting the government or someone else to take care of them. That's not the case. Seventy-six percent of single mothers work and provide for their own children. Eighty-five percent of single fathers work and provide for their own children. They aren't waiting for someone else to come in and meet their children's needs.

As the church, we must get beyond the myths so that we can minister to single parents in the way that we should. Within the community and our own homes, we must stop condemning them and instead come alongside them in a powerful way to help them. We know how much most single parents accomplish while rearing their children on their own. Just imagine how much more could be done if they and their children were surrounded by a circle of support with loving hearts and willing hands, pitching in to help make a difference. I pray to God that it becomes so.

CHAPTER 1

THE FIRST SINGLE PARENT: YOU ARE NOT FORGOTTEN

> Early the next morning Abraham took some food and
> a skin of water and gave them to Hagar. He set them
> on her shoulders and then sent her off with the boy.
> She went on her way and wandered in the Desert of
> Beersheba. When the water in the skin was gone,
> she put the boy under one of the bushes. Then she
> went off and sat down about a bowshot away, for she
> thought, "I cannot watch the boy die." And as she sat
> there, she began to sob. God heard the boy crying,
> and the angel of God called to Hagar from heaven.
>
> (Genesis 21:14-17a)

FORCED INTO SINGLE PARENTING

In order to begin to better understand single parents and their situations, we will use this incident from Genesis 21 as a backdrop. In this chapter, we meet an Egyptian woman named Hagar—a woman of color, perhaps a Black woman—whom we view as a single parent worried about having to take care of her teenage son on her own. But it hadn't always been like that. Initially Hagar and her man, Abraham, were raising this boy together. They had a roof over their heads and all of the resources they needed. The boy's father was caring for him, providing for him, and giving him direction. All of that was in place.

Even though polygamy was a common practice during this time in history, the first wife of this man pressured him to get rid of his own son and the boy's mother. Sarah told Abraham, "Get rid of that slave woman and her son, for that woman's son will never share in the inheritance with my son Isaac" (Genesis 21:10). Abraham did as she said, thereby forcing Hagar into the role of a single parent.

We would have thought that Abraham would have stood up to Sarah and denied her demands. We would have expected him to man up in this situation and tell her, "This is *my* son. *I* brought him into the world, and I'm going to take care of him. *I* am responsible for him and his welfare, so I am going to take care of my responsibilities."

But that isn't what happened. In so many instances, even in the twenty-first century, this pattern that Abraham set still continues. The pressure that comes from family members and friends is just too much for these men. So, rather than embrace the responsibilities involved with raising their children, they just kick them out of their lives and leave it to the children's mothers to care for them and meet their needs. Instead of manning up and being the fathers they are supposed to be, they forsake their own children just to please these other voices.

So now, Hagar was facing her new reality. She was cast out of her home, forced to leave a place of stability and security, driven away from all the people she knew, and told that it would be up to her to care for her son alone. We can only imagine how devastated she felt. But one thing I love about Hagar is that she didn't use her single-parent status as an excuse for being a *bad* parent.

AN EXAMPLE, NOT AN EXCUSE

A crucial thing to recognize is that the number of parents in the home is not as important as it is to have one *good* parent in the home. There are children today growing up in homes with the desired two parents, but not even one *good* parent to protect them, nurture them, provide for them, and direct them in life. Having two parents in the home is not an assurance that children will receive good parenting. And finding oneself in the role of a single parent is never an excuse for being a *bad* parent.

Every parent must bring up children with a God-consciousness — an awareness that there is a God and that God loves them and has created them for a purpose. *Every* parent must provide love, nurturing, and emotional support for the children. *Every* parent must supply a roof over their heads, food to eat, and clothes to wear. *Every* parent must know the friends they keep and where they are at any given moment. *Every* parent must set boundaries for their children so that they learn what is right and wrong, safe and unsafe, acceptable and unacceptable. *Every* parent must administer wise and loving discipline for their children's sake because Proverbs 13:24 says, "Whoever spares the rod hates their children, but the one who loves their children is careful to discipline them." *Every* parent must "Train up a child in the way he should go," because Proverbs 22:6 (KJV) promises, "And when he is old, he will not depart from it." All of these things have nothing to do with the number of parents in a home. They are merely aspects of *good* parenting, and they must happen whether the parent raises the children with a partner or alone.

Rather than becoming an excuse for single parents, Hagar became an example. That's my encouragement to single parents everywhere: become the good parents that God wants you to be. My friend Julia Carson, who has now gone to be with the Lord, did just that. She testified that she had been a teenage girl with two children and no husband, but she didn't use her situation as an excuse for what she couldn't do. Instead, she accepted her responsibilities by working a variety of jobs to support her family, attending Martin University, and then finishing up her education at Indiana University-Purdue University at Indianapolis. As a secretary in her new job at a union hall, she did her work with such excellence that she was noticed and hired away by a newly elected congressman to work in his office in Indianapolis. Seven years later, her hard work, abilities, intellect, and wonderful personality prompted this congressman to encourage *her* to run for office.

After Julia was elected to the Indiana House of Representatives, where she served for four years, she then won a seat in the Indiana

Senate, where she stayed for fourteen years. Next, she was elected a township trustee and kept that post for six years. When her former boss retired from the U.S. House of Representatives, Julia ran as his replacement and won the election, making her the first Black congresswoman from Indiana. In all of her years in politics, she never lost an election. And the truly great thing about Julia Carson is that she always worked on behalf of the least, the lonely, and the left-out. She supported veterans, single parents, senior citizens, and the homeless.

Even though Julia spent part of her time living and working in Washington, her heart was always at home—in Indiana. She never forgot her roots nor abandoned her family. In fact, when her grandson André was fourteen years old and needed somebody to take him in, Julia again accepted the role of single parent by raising her grandson. She did pretty well, too. He is now *Congressman* André Carson. If we were able to ask Julia, "How did you do that? How did you manage all of that?" she would respond, "Through my relationship with God, by His Son Jesus Christ and the power of the Holy Spirit." Through God, Julia Carson didn't just survive; she thrived. She didn't offer excuses; she became an example.

That was true of Hagar, too. She was raising a teenage boy with no help from the boy's father. Yet she and her son went beyond just surviving. They thrived. The question that immediately comes to our minds is, "How did she do that?"

WE HAVE TO MOVE ON

Hagar learned that there are times when we have to move on. When she realized things weren't going to work out between her and her child's father, she didn't hang around, stalking him. She didn't show up on his job. She didn't slash the wheels on his chariot. She didn't text him or try to reach out to him on social media every five minutes. Instead of doing all that, she simply moved on. When her baby's daddy betrayed her, she moved on. When her baby's daddy kicked her out, she moved on. When her baby's daddy was no longer willing to be in a relationship with them, she moved on.

That's what we've got to do sometimes. We've got to move on. We've got to move on socially, move on emotionally, move on mentally, and move on physically. When we see that the life we envisioned for ourselves and our children is not going to happen, we can't *will* it into existence. We can't *make* someone love us. But that's a hard fact to face. It hurts deeply to see a love we shared with someone slowly fade away. Experiencing rejection is like someone stabbing a knife through the heart. It challenges our faith because we really believed that God was in this relationship. It challenges our image of ourselves because we don't see ourselves as quitters. It challenges our understanding of human nature. We always think that if we do a little more, try a little harder, and be a little better, it just has to work out. But sometimes it doesn't. In her song "Blame It on Me," Chrisette Michele helps us to realize that there sometimes comes a time that we've got to move on:

> Yes, I love you, but I really got to lose you
> Freedom is where I want to be
> Yes, I'll probably always love you
> But I'm moving
> I got to do this for me

Sometimes, we've just got to move on. If we are to have any respect for ourselves; if we are to be a positive role model for our children; if we are to have any hope of living a beautiful life that is real as opposed to an unfulfilling fantasy, we've got to move on.

Hagar came to the realization that, "Abraham doesn't want me. And if my son's father doesn't want me, I don't want him." A relationship can only work out if *you* want the person who wants *you*. When you want someone who doesn't want you, it can't work. When someone wants you, but you don't want that person, it can't work.

Hagar understood that the only thing that is permanent is what we have with God. Everything else is temporary. The relationship we have with God through His Son Jesus Christ is permanent. Everything else is temporary. We have to stop trying to make something permanent that God knew would be only temporary. Our friendships, our relationships, our partnerships are all temporary.

31

We are in those for a reason and a season. When the reason and the season is over, we've got to move on.

PERMANENT OR TEMPORARY?

Recently, I heard my little niece talking about how she needed to get a perm. I said, "Baby, you just said a couple months ago that you were going to get a permanent. Now you're saying you've got to get another one?" "Yeah, I got to go get another one." "But if you got a permanent two months ago, and you need another permanent today, that was not a *permanent*. That was a *temporary*." We have to stop thinking something is a "permanent" when it is only a "temporary."

Radio personality Donna Schiele was hosting a call-in show one day on the subject of tattoos. That general topic turned into a conversation about putting someone's name in a tattoo on our bodies. One young woman was talking about how she got a tattoo with her boyfriend's name because, she said, "I *love* him." Donna Schiele said, "I'm not tattooing any man's name on my body—not even my husband's—because I only know one person who will love me unconditionally, and that is Jesus."

Now, let's not pretend that we're not like that young girl who called the show. There is undoubtedly someone reading this book right now who has "David" tattooed on her arm, but her current boyfriend's name is "Kevin." In fact, I did my own research on this topic. I went to a restaurant in the neighborhood around our church in Indianapolis. The young girl who came over to serve me had "Robert" tattooed on her neck. I had never met her before, but when I saw the tattoo, I asked her, "How are you and Robert doing?"

"Well, we ain't together no more. We broke up."

"Well, why do you still have his name on your neck?"

"I'm trying to save enough money to have it removed."

She had made the same mistake that a lot of us make. She tried to make something permanent when it was only temporary.

Sᴇx Wᴏɴ'ᴛ Mᴀᴋᴇ Hɪᴍ Lᴏᴠᴇ Yᴏᴜ

One thing that helped Hagar *move* on is that she didn't *add* on. She didn't have a second child by her son's father in an attempt to hang on to that man. She realized that a second child would not cause him to ask her to move in with him. For her, it was not about moving *in*, but moving *on*. And she knew that it would become much harder to move on if she kept adding on.

Women, don't think that sex is going to chain a man, or having a baby is going to bind a man to you. Oftentimes, that man has already had a baby by another woman before he had a baby with you—and she couldn't keep him either. Having two or three babies isn't going to keep him with you. You've got to move on.

Remember the story of Leah in Genesis 29? Leah loved a man named Jacob, but Jacob loved Rachel. Jacob had agreed to work seven years for Laban, Rachel's father, in exchange for Rachel's hand in marriage. In those days, an engagement established that these two people belonged to each other; in fact, it was just as if they were legally married. Then at an appointed time, a marriage feast was held to celebrate the couple's union. Soon afterward, they would consummate their marriage as they began their life together.

On the night of the marriage feast for Jacob and Rachel, Jacob had been eating and drinking at his father-in-law's table. When the time came for Jacob and Rachel to be alone and consummate their marriage, Laban sent Leah instead of Rachel into Jacob's dark tent. Even though Leah knew Jacob was in love with her sister, she loved Jacob, and, in order to try to manipulate him, she went along with her father's plan. She hid her identity and presented herself as someone she wasn't, tricking Jacob into having sex with her. He went to bed that night thinking he was with the woman he loved. He had spent seven years dreaming about this night. He was passionate in expressing his love to her. He held her tenderly in his arms all night. This was the night he had been waiting for. But then, as it says in Genesis 29:25, "When morning came, there was Leah!" We can only imagine his shock, disbelief, anger, and feelings of betrayal.

Laban had him in a bind at this point. He told Jacob to finish that week out with Leah, and then he would also give him Rachel, for whom he was required to work yet another seven years. So Jacob, who had expected to begin his long awaited married life with the woman of his dreams, instead wound up with two wives—one whom he loved and another whom he didn't. While most Bible versions say that Leah was unloved, some versions, such as the King James, go so far as to say that Jacob *hated* Leah.

Get the full impact of this situation. That first night, Jacob was tricked into having sex with Leah, so he behaved towards her with all the love and tenderness that he intended to show Rachel. But after that, Leah knew that Jacob didn't love her. *Jacob* knew that he didn't love her. All their friends knew that Jacob didn't love her. All her family knew that Jacob didn't love her. So why did he continue to have sex with her? Why did he keep going to bed with a woman he didn't love? Was he satisfied just with having sex without any thought about Leah as a person? Was it just like two dogs copulating—with no respect or love, just acting on instinct?

The sad fact is that some men *will* have sex with a woman without thinking anything about her—without any regard for her feelings or any respect for her as a person. They act solely on instinct, just as a male dog that meets a female dog in heat. If one of his friends hears about such a man being with a particular woman, the man is quick to respond, "Oh, she ain't my woman. We were just having sex."

To these men, sex is just an activity they enjoy, a form of entertainment, a pleasure in which they indulge whenever they get the chance. Sometimes it's even a game to see how many women they can get, or at its worst, a vengeful act of power. It has nothing to do with who the woman is. She is just a means to an end, a thing they can use and then toss aside.

It doesn't matter what these men are *saying* in order to get women in bed with them. Those are just words they've said so many times that they roll off their tongues as though they were saying their ABCs. Women need to know that there *are* men like that out there, so it takes time to find out whether a man in whom she's interested is one of the good guys—or one of the bad guys. A woman needs to make sure a deep and respectful relationship comes before the sex. In order to do that, she must find out if his love is giving and enduring. And then she needs to make sure the wedding ring that means forever comes before the sex.

But Leah didn't wait for her own man. She thought she could have the man who was in love with her sister. We can only imagine what it would be like for a woman to have sex with a man who doesn't love her. And then for him to get up from her bed and go home to make love to the woman he really loves must leave her with a deep ache inside, along with feelings of worthlessness and an emptiness that no amount of pretending can fill.

Babies Won't Keep Him with You

In Leah's situation, hope appeared for her when she found that she was carrying Jacob's baby. Genesis 29:32 says, "Leah became pregnant and gave birth to a son. She named him Reuben, for she said, 'It is because the Lord has seen my misery. Surely my husband will love me now.' " She thought this baby was going to bring Jacob's love to her. She named him Reuben, which means, "See, a son." But she might as well have been saying, "See *me*, Jacob. See *me*. Look what I did. See, I have value. See, I have worth. Look at me. Get your eyes off Rachel and look at me." But it didn't work because Jacob still loved Rachel.

So Leah added on. She thought having another child would surely make a difference, so she got pregnant and gave birth to a second son. Genesis 29:33 records, "She conceived again, and when she gave birth to a son she said, 'Because the Lord heard that I am not loved, he gave me this one too.' So she named him Simeon." The name Simeon comes from a word that means "hear." Not only was Leah saying that the Lord heard her plight and gave her another son, but she was probably also saying to Jacob, "Hear me, Jacob. Hear *me*. Hear how I feel. Hear *my* heart. Know who I am." But Jacob wasn't listening. He had no eyes for Leah, and he had no ears to hear her.

Still Leah added on. Genesis 29:34 tells us, "Again she conceived, and when she gave birth to a son she said, 'Now at last my husband will become attached to me, because I have borne him three sons.' So he was named Levi." The name Levi means "attached."

Leah thought that this third son would undoubtedly bring about Jacob's attachment to her. She must have thought, "He *has* to love me now. I've given him three sons. Surely, these sons will bind my husband to me. I've waited a long time, but it will be worth it. Jacob will be mine now."

My question to Leah would have been this: "How many babies does it take? How many babies do you have to bear to get this man to love you?" But Leah wasn't thinking about that absurdity. Instead, she had yet a fourth son. But there was a difference this time. Leah no longer expected anything from Jacob because she had borne yet another son. Instead, Genesis 29:35 says, "She conceived again, and when she gave birth to a son she said, 'This time I will praise the Lord.' So she named him Judah. Then she stopped having children." The name of Judah means "praise." This time, she moved her attention away from Jacob and toward God. At this moment, she was no longer seeking anything from Jacob. She didn't ask him again to see her, hear her, or attach himself to her. She stopped looking at the man and began looking at God.

But Leah couldn't keep her focus on the Lord. She couldn't stop wanting what was never rightfully hers. She couldn't stop wanting what she could never have. Pathetically, she spent all her life trying to win Jacob's love. When Leah felt that she could no longer bear children herself, she gave him her servant for sex and procreation. Eventually she was able to have more children, but even with her sixth son, she was saying, "This time my husband will treat me with honor, because I have borne him six sons" (Genesis 30:20). Leah, wake up! No matter how many babies you have, Jacob isn't going to love you!

TRANSFORMING DISADVANTAGE INTO ADVANTAGE

Now, Hagar had a different spirit and outlook than Leah. She knew that in order to move on, she had to stop adding on. She knew that it wouldn't matter how many children she had with Abraham; he was never going to love her anyway because he loved Sarah. No amount of children was ever going to change that, so Hagar didn't try. Instead, she could move on because she learned to take what was a *dis*advantage and turn it to her son's advantage.

It's a disadvantage when a father is not in a son's life; when a father puts his children's mother out; when a father is not a role model for his son; when a father won't support his child financially; and when a father separates himself not only from a woman but from his children as well. All of these things that Abraham did created a disadvantage for Hagar and her son. But this single mother was determined to turn it into an *ad*vantage.

Hagar's role in Abraham's household was that of a bondservant to Abraham's wife. Being a bondservant meant she was in bond*age*. As long as she stayed in Abraham's home, even though she was technically his woman, she would always be in bondage. But when he put her out of his home, she was no longer enslaved. She was free. Her disadvantage—being put out of her home—became her advantage, her way to freedom.

During the times in which Hagar lived, women were treated as property by the men. She literally was the property of her baby's father. Whatever her view was about parenting, it never counted. It was always her baby's father's opinion about parenting that meant anything. Whatever she said as the mother of her child could be overridden by his father. What she said didn't count. Anything she said was always a suggestion, not a decision. But when Abraham put her out, not only does her view count, it's the *only* view that counts. Not only does her word count, it's the *only* word that counts. Now when she speaks, it isn't a suggestion, but a decision. As a parent, she had to take her disadvantage, turn it into an advantage, and use it for the welfare of her child.

CHANGE OF ADDRESS

Some women in the twenty-first century don't like to be transparent about what they are dealing with as single parents because they know that some of us will judge them, condemn them, or put them down. If one of them came to us and tried to be open and transparent, we wouldn't know how to address her issues, so we would just start harassing her or making her feel bad. Or sometimes we throw sympathy on a single mother that she doesn't need or want: "Oh, I feel so sorry for you. If you had stayed with him, he would really take care of you." We don't understand that she is turning her disadvantage into an advantage and moving on.

I went to school in Dallas and I go back to that city multiple times every year to preach. I really know that place, especially all the restaurants where I like to eat. One day when I was there, I was trying to make a quick run to a Red Lobster, but it wasn't there anymore. It had been there for twenty years, but it was gone. I began thinking that the economy there must be really bad for it to lose a restaurant that is part of a chain. So I talked to my smartphone and asked where the closest Red Lobster was. It informed me that the restaurant was only about a mile and a half away. What I found out that day is that the Red Lobster I knew hadn't gone out of business; it just moved to a new location.

Single mothers, there's a lesson from this Red Lobster that you have to help us understand. When one of us comes up to you and starts pouring out the sympathy ("Oh, baby, I was so sorry to hear what happened"), don't let us go on. Stop us and say, "Oh, no, I'm fine. I'm not out of business. I just moved to a new location." And when folks try to get you to talk about the child's father in front of your child, just say, "Oh, no, I've moved on from that." Don't let us think you are psychologically dependent on that man and that you can't go on without him. You didn't go out of business; you just moved to a new location. If you are going to survive and thrive, you have to move on.

WE NEED ONE ANOTHER

If you are going to survive and thrive, you have to listen up. It was an angel of God who spoke to Hagar from heaven. Many of us can't get the answer we need because we won't listen. Too many of us are trying so hard to prove to everybody that we don't need anybody, we will listen to nobody. But God did not plan for any parent to raise a child alone. Even if the other parent isn't there, you don't have to do this by yourself.

38

The Bible talks about the body of Christ. Galatians 6:1 says that we are to restore another person "gently," and it tells us in verse 2 that we are to "carry one another's burdens." We are supposed to do this thing called life *together*. Every believer has at least one spiritual gift to be used for the building up of the body. God never intended for us to do it by ourselves. Ephesians 4:16 says, "From [Christ] the whole body, joined and held together by every supporting ligament, grows and builds itself up in love, as each part does its work." God designed His church for us to work together, to love and be loved. We need to learn to both give and receive.

ANGELS IN OUR MIDST

We have to be willing to listen because we never know when God might send an angel to speak to us, even as one spoke to Hagar. God always knows how to send an angel at just the right time. Just when we think it is over, just when we think nothing can happen to help us, just when we think there is no way out of our mess, that's when God's angel shows up. It was after Hagar had no water left to give her son to drink and she believed he was going to die that the angel appeared to her.

"In the year that King Uzziah died," begins Isaiah 6:1, God sent seraphim, another type of angel, to speak to Isaiah. When Moses was leading the Israelites into Canaan, God said to him, as recorded in Exodus 23:20-21a, "See, I am sending an angel ahead of you to guard you along the way and to bring you to the place I have prepared. Pay attention to him and listen to what he says." When the angel appears, we've got to listen.

When Daniel was in the lions' den and people thought there was no way he could escape, God sent an angel to close the mouths of the lions so that Daniel was protected. After Daniel's night in the lions' den, King Darius "called to Daniel in an anguished voice, 'Daniel, servant of the living God, has your God, whom you serve continually, been able to rescue you from the lions?'" (Daniel 6:20). Daniel's response was, "My God sent his angel, and he shut the mouths of the lions. They have not hurt me" (v. 22).

An angel had appeared to Mary to let her know that she was to be the vessel through which God would bring His Son into the world. But Joseph, the man to whom she was pledged to be married, was not there when that happened. All he knew was that they had not yet consummated their relationship and yet one day it became obvious that Mary was pregnant. He loved her and didn't want to publicly humiliate her. Being a righteous man, however, he felt compelled to follow the Mosaic law, so he was going to divorce her quietly. "But after he had considered this, an angel of the Lord appeared to him in a dream and said, 'Joseph, son of David, do not be afraid to take Mary home as your wife, because what is conceived in her is from the Holy Spirit. She will give birth to a son, and you are to give him the name Jesus, because he will save his people from their sins'" (Matthew 1:20-21). God sent an angel on Mary's behalf.

Jesus had fasted in the wilderness for forty days. Hungry, tired, and weak, He was then confronted three times by the devil, who tempted Him to turn stones into bread, to jump down off the temple, and to bow down and worship him. Jesus withstood the temptations by quoting Scriptures to him and letting him know that He was going do things God's way and no other. After all of this, "Then the devil left him, and angels came and attended him" (Matthew 4:11).

When Jesus was born, there were shepherds watching their flocks in a field that night, and, according to Luke 2:9-15:

> An angel of the Lord appeared to them, and the glory of the Lord shone around them, and they were terrified. But the angel said to them, "Do not be afraid. I bring you good news that will cause great joy for all the people. Today in the town of David a Savior has been born to you; he is the Messiah, the Lord. This will be a sign to you: You will find a baby wrapped in cloths and lying in a manger." Suddenly a great company of the heavenly host appeared with the angel, praising God and saying, "Glory to God in the highest heaven, and on earth peace to those on whom his favor rests." When the angels had left them and gone into heaven, the shepherds said to one another, "Let's go to Bethlehem and see this thing that has happened, which the Lord has told us about."

God couldn't keep such wonderful news to Himself. Jesus, His Son, was born into the world, and He wanted *everyone* to know about it. Even the angels themselves were excited. One angel came to tell the shepherds the good news, and suddenly, a whole army of heavenly beings was on the scene praising God and joining in the telling of the good news. All of heaven was overflowing with joy and excitement. God knows when to send His angels.

After Jesus was crucified, when the women got to the tomb, found the stone had been rolled away, and saw the body of Jesus was gone, they were wondering what could have happened to their Lord. But two angels appeared and said to them, "Why do you look for the living among the dead? He is not here; he has risen!" (Luke 24:5).

LISTEN TO THE "ANGELS"!

Grandma said, "All day and all night, angels keep a watch over me." God will send an angel. Sometimes the angel might be called Gabriel, sometimes Michael, sometimes one with another name, but He still sends an angel. Sometimes it might be called Mommy or Daddy, sometimes sister or brother, sometimes teacher or principal, sometimes pastor or minister, sometimes neighbor or friend. Angels appear in many different forms, yet God sends His angels at just the right time. But you've got to listen to the angels when they come.

Hagar was in such a mess and a hard place, but she still listened to the angel that appeared to her. Had it been some of us, we would have said, "I'm not listening to you. Have you ever been a single parent? Have you ever been homeless and broke? Have you ever been in a bad relationship?" We would have missed the opportunity because the angel would have responded, "No, I've never been a single parent, homeless, broke, or in a bad relationship." And we would have said, "Well, you don't have anything to say to me." We would have missed the angel's counsel because our minds were already closed.

We must realize that someone can minister to us even though he or she hasn't been in our same situation. If we are in a hospital in intensive care and need a blood transfusion, we're not going to be looking for that blood to come from the patient in the next room to ours. We're going to look for someone healthy, someone whose blood is not contaminated with disease and bacteria. No one has to be in our predicament to get a word to us that can help us. An angel is a messenger of God, who has been in the presence of God, and who has word from God. We can't listen to everybody, but we can listen to the angels. They may not have gone through what we've gone through or have been in the same experience that we're in, but if they have been in the presence of God and they come with a word from God, there is power in that word.

Look at what the angel said to Hagar. He spoke to her about fear, faith, the physical needs of her child, and the future. The angel called Hagar by name and told her not to be afraid: "What is the matter, Hagar? Do not be afraid" (Genesis 21:17). The angel found Hagar in the wilderness, homeless after being thrown out of her house by Abraham—with a crying child and not even any water left. She had every reason to be afraid, but she had one reason not to fear: her faith in God. It was her faith that was able to trump everything that was going wrong in her life.

We all go through difficult situations. There are times when, like Hagar, we feel hopeless and feel like giving up. But it is just at those moments that our faith can drive out our fear. Repeatedly in the Bible, God tells us to *fear not*. No matter what circumstance you are in, and no matter how long the situation lasts, God's *fear nots* will get you through.

CHILD SUPPORT, NOT MOTHER SUPPORT

There is a particular detail for us to notice as we are looking at all the things about which the angel talked to Hagar. One thing the angel did *not* talk about was the child's father. The angel showed up with a word from God and that word said nothing at all about the child's father. Let me be very clear. Father's should be held accountable for the needs and care of their children. We have a system now that mothers did not have in biblical times. Our judicial system allows mothers to take fathers to court if they are not willingly paying child support.

But Hagar did not have that option. If she had, there would surely have been another verse somewhere that would have read, "Now Hagar went to the prosecutor's office with a paternity test and said, 'Abraham is the father of my child. He had been taking care of him, but now he has kicked us out, so I need for you to garnishee his wages so that I can take care of my son.'" We don't see anything like that, however, because there was nothing like that in Hagar's time.

But even though we do have such things in place in our time, we sometimes hear single women saying, "I'm not getting anything from my baby's father, and I don't care! I don't want anything from that man! I don't want him doing anything. I don't want any check from him. I don't want him in my child's life. I don't want *anything* from him!" I would remind those women that the financial support isn't for them. That's why it is called "*child* support." It isn't called "*mother* support." Take that money. Use it for the child. Put it in a trust fund for the child. It is *for* the child. That man is just as responsible for this child as you are, so make sure he accepts that responsibility and you use the support for its intended purpose.

I also want to celebrate those fathers who handle their business with their children. I praise God for the men who provide for their children, nurture them, and show them they are loved. I thank God for every man who didn't divorce his children when he divorced his wife, and for every man who didn't break up with his children when he broke up with his girlfriend. It's the irresponsible fathers who make the rest of us look bad. It is those who abandon their children and do nothing to meet their needs that reflect negatively on men in general.

FOCUS ON THE GIVENS

But when the angel talked to Hagar, he didn't say anything about the father, or what the father was going to do or not do. He didn't say anything to Hagar about Abraham's character or what God thought of him. He didn't talk to the mother about how to make the father better. He talked to the mother about how to make the *mother* better. Some women waste ten or fifteen years or more trying to make their child's father right—time that would have been better spent in making themselves right.

For single fathers, it's the same principle. Don't waste time trying to get the mother to do what she should be doing. You are not responsible for her and what she does, but only for yourself and what you do. The solution to your problem is not in your child's other parent. Hagar's solution was not in Abraham. That's why the angel never brought his name up. He wasn't part of her solution.

Now, I'm no longer good at math. When I was in school, I used to be good at that subject. I was especially good at algebra. I knew the vocabulary (expressions, variables, coefficients, constants, factors, and all that) and how to solve equations. But, as they say, "Use it or lose it." Well, I've lost it. But one thing I do know is that when we have our "givens" in algebra, we had better not pick up some variable from somewhere else that has nothing to do with the equation we're working. Otherwise, we can never come to the right solution.

Look at the equation: $3x + 8 = 14$. If I'm going to solve for "x," I have to look at the givens in front of me. I can't pull something from somewhere else. I can't bring in a variable that has nothing to do with this equation. I can't pretend something is there when it isn't. That's why some folks flunk algebra: they don't use the givens to come to the right solution.

In the same way, the father in Genesis 21 was not one of the givens. He was not part of the equation because he was not there. So, to come to the right solution, Hagar could not bring the father into the equation. We are reluctant to accept that, at least in part, because we continually hear that if the father is not present in the home, the child is doomed to failure. I've heard the same things, read the same reports, and seen the same statistics. But I've come to the conclusion that it's not about how many parents are in the house, but whether or not there is a *good* parent in the house. There can be two *bad* parents in the home, and they will still not know how to help their child succeed. But one *good* parent—especially one who prays for the child and seeks God for guidance in caring for that child—can help a child to grow into positive, responsible adulthood just fine. With the help and helpers God provides along the way, one *good* parent can get the job done.

"OMAHA!"

Keep in mind that good parents are always listening to an "angel"—someone with a word from God to help them feel supported and stay on track. Before beginning this study on single parenthood, I fasted, prayed, and listened to God so that I would have something of value to pass along to single parents who feel frustrated, angry, confused, and alone. No, I have never been a single parent. But I have been in God's presence, and I have been in God's Word. And there is value in the Word of God.

On February 2, 2014, at the Super Bowl in East Rutherford, New Jersey, Peyton Manning had a word that he used when hiking the football: "Omaha! Omaha! Omaha!" Only his teammates and coaches know what that word means. People have speculated, but Manning has purposely sidestepped answering questions about his word.

Manning used "Omaha!" repeatedly during the AFC championship game and led his team to victory. Not only that, but that word had other value as well. Omaha Steaks and other Omaha-based companies decided to use it as a marketing ploy. They said that during the AFC championship game, they would offer eight hundred dollars to Manning's favorite charity every time he yelled out, "Omaha!" He called it out thirty-one times, and earned $24,800 for charity! That word had value. At the Super Bowl, the Omaha Chamber of Commerce and other corporations got into the spirit and, even though Manning could only be heard saying it twice during that game, they donated over $67,000 to Manning's PeyBack Foundation to assist at-risk youth. His word had value.

What's especially interesting is that Manning has said that he was not the first to use the word "Omaha" in a game. He said the Denver Broncos were using that word even before he got on the team. When he got there, they gave him a word, and he started using it. Just look at the value attached to the word that someone else gave him. In the same way, God's Word was here before you got here, and His Word will be here when you're gone. But when you take God's Word and speak it into your situation, everything is going to be alright.

KEEP YOUR EYES OPEN

If you are going to survive and thrive, you not only have to move on and listen up, but you also have to open up. Genesis 21:19 says, "God opened her eyes." And after Hagar's eyes were open, "she saw a well of water." Remember that Hagar and her son were in the wilderness. The little bit of water the father provided as he sent them away was gone. Hagar had no one to turn to. She had no options. She saw that her beloved son was going to die and she was helpless to stop it from happening. She put the little boy under some bushes, and then she went about a hundred yards away so that she would not have to watch him die. Then "she began to sob" (v. 16).

But then came the angel with a word from God. And after Hagar listened to the angel, "God opened her eyes and she saw a well of water. She went, and filled the skin with water, and gave the boy a drink" (v. 19). Notice that the well of water didn't suddenly appear. It had been there all along, but Hagar was too worried, too depressed, and in too much pain to see it. God had already put the solution to her problem in place. But she couldn't see it until God opened her eyes.

This is too often true in our situations as well. Our loving God sees what we are going through and puts a solution in place for us. But we are not looking with the eyes of faith. We are looking only with eyes that see the problem, not the solution. We are focused on how bad the situation is, how much worse it is getting with every passing minute, and how hopeless it is. We cry as one who is alone with no hope in sight. We are oblivious to the fact that God has already put our solution in place.

Mary experienced something similar to this when she went to the tomb where Jesus lay and found that the stone had been rolled away and His body was gone. She "stood weeping outside the tomb" (John 20:11). When she peered in, she saw two angels who asked her why she was crying. She sobbed, "They have taken my Lord away . . . and I don't know where they have put him" (v. 13). Jesus appeared to Mary, but, just as Hagar could not see the very thing she yearned for, Mary could not see Jesus. Through her tears, pain, and despondency, she saw only a "gardener." Even when He spoke, her ears were as closed as her eyes, and she could not recognize

His voice. But then, "Jesus said to her, 'Mary'" (v. 16). Suddenly, she saw that Jesus was with her. The very One she yearned for was already at her side.

What Is God Saying?

Often we fail to look to God when we are in the midst of a major problem. Instead of believing God, we falter; instead of crying to God, we just cry; instead of opening our eyes to look for God's solution, we close our eyes and wait for the worst to happen. We cannot see what God has provided if we are not looking to Him. We *must* open ourselves to God. We have to stop tripping over our past and crying over our present. We have to open ourselves to God and claim His promises for our future.

Look at what God promised Hagar for her son: "I will make him into a great nation" (Genesis 21:18). If you are reading this right now as a single parent, God wants you to hear Him say the same words of hope about your child. God can make *your* son or *your* daughter great. God said to Hagar, "I will . . . ." If God says to you that He *will*, it doesn't matter who *won't*. If God *wills* it so, He has the power to *make* it so. Even if the earthly father *won't*, the heavenly Father *will*. If the earthly parent steps out, God steps in.

God said, "I will make him . . . ." If God has to "make" a child into something, that means the child isn't that way already. So, we must not give up on our children. A son or daughter doesn't already have to be what God is going to make of him or her. God said, "*I* will make . . . " There are countless Christians, myself included, who can remember that what we *were* is not what we *are* now. God made us who we are today.

God said that He would make Hagar's son "great." As the son of the wealthy and prestigious Abraham, he would have possibly have been considered "great" if he had stayed in his father's home where he bore his father's name and had access to all that his father could have given him. But God didn't have to have all that. God was not dependent on Abraham to accomplish what He wanted to accomplish in this boy's life. God can make a boy or a girl *great* with or without a parent in his or her life. It's up to God to decide who is going to be great.

GOD DID IT!

Before I began writing this book on single parenting, I brought together fifteen single mothers to hear what they had to say. I didn't want to be wrong about what I was thinking or miss the mark in knowing how to help single parents, so I brought in real single parents with real children to hear what was on their hearts. As I opened the meeting with them, I asked them to tell me their real challenges and issues. I asked them to be open and transparent with me. I told them that *I* wasn't going to speak to *them*, but I wanted *them* to speak to *me*. I wanted them to inform and enlighten me.

For the next two hours, they shared with me their challenges, victories, and defeats. Sometimes they were crying, sometimes silent. Sometimes they were worried and concerned, sometimes very confident. This went on for two hours. By the end of our time together, we were all in tears. It was a very moving experience. Even though I had told them that I wasn't going to speak but merely listen to them, as we were closing, they said, "Pastor, you've got to say *something* to us. You've got to tell us *something*. You can't let us just leave here without saying *something* to help us."

So I shared my testimony with them. I reminded them that I am the product of a single-parent home. My father left the house when I was eight years old and never came back. He never showed up at any of my ball games, never showed up at my school, never showed up for graduations, never showed up with money to care for my needs. He was absent from my life. He never did anything for my mother or any of us four children. Nothing. I was the product of that situation—a broken home and dysfunctional family.

I told the women that I wanted them to understand that I love the Lord with all my heart. I have a relationship with God through the Lord Jesus Christ. God's Spirit lives inside of me, and I minister to people all over the country and in other places in the world. I have been married to the same woman for twenty-seven years. I have four sons. I am in their lives, and they are in my life. I have a wonderful life. So, I said to the women, "My word to you is that your children are going to be fine." But I realized later on that I had misspoken. God's word to Hagar was not that her child would be "fine," but that her child would be "great." God didn't say that He would make her child okay or fine, alright or average. No, God said that He would make him *great*. True to God's word, Ishmael grew to be a great man, a great hunter, with great skills, a great wife, a great family, and he went on to become a great nation. And the only testimony Hagar had was that God did it!

When I was a young man, I used to be invited by youth groups, schools, and churches to come and give my testimony. They asked me to share how I went from being a mixed-up kid in a broken home—without the money to have what other kids had, with no father to guide me into manhood, angry and not knowing I was angry—to being an honor roll student in high school, continuing on to college, getting a degree, finding a good wife, and entering the work that God chose for me. They wanted me to share how I did all that.

My conclusion, my testimony, had to be the same as Hagar's, the same as Ishmael's, and the same as my mother's: God did it! And just as God opened doors and worked miracles in the life of this fatherless kid in Indianapolis, Indiana, so also God can work miracles for your sons and daughters. That same God who sent a word of hope and promise to the distraught mother in Genesis is here today to speak a word of hope and promise to you.

God,

> *We know that what You have done in the past for others, You will do in the present for us. We know that You care about Your children and Your children's children. We know that if we listen to You and obey You, You will make our children great. But God, this is a crazy, mixed-up world, and we don't always know just what to do or just what to say. We need You. We need Your wisdom, guidance, and protection. Watch over our families and hold our children*

in the palm of Your hand. Help us to keep our eyes open to see You and our ears open to hear Your voice. Encourage us when we are down, and strengthen us for the task before us. Heavenly Father, teach us to be good parents to our *children even as You are to us. And when others, knowing our circumstances, see good things when they look at us and our children, and they ask how this is possible, let us be ever faithful in proclaiming to them, "GOD did it!" In Christ's name we pray, Amen.*

CHAPTER 2

A FRUSTRATED SINGLE PARENT: FINDING FOCUS

Some time later two prostitutes came to the king to have an argument settled. "Please, my lord," one of them began, "this woman and I live in the same house. I gave birth to a baby while she was with me in the house. Three days later this woman also had a baby. We were alone; there were only two of us in the house. "But her baby died during the night when she rolled over on it. Then she got up in the night and took my son from beside me while I was asleep. She laid her dead child in my arms and took mine to sleep beside her. And in the morning when I tried to nurse my son, he was dead! But when I looked more closely in the morning light, I saw that it wasn't my son at all." Then the other woman interrupted, "It certainly was your son, and the living child is mine." "No," the first woman said, "the living child is mine, and the dead one is yours." And so they argued back and forth before the king.

Then the king said, "Let's get the facts straight. Both of you claim the living child is yours, and each says that the dead one belongs to the other. All right, bring me a sword." So a sword was brought to the king. Then he said, "Cut the living child in two, and give half to one woman and half to the other!" Then the woman who was the real mother of the living child, and who loved him very much, cried out, "Oh no, my lord! Give her the child—please do not kill him!" But the other woman said, "All right, he will be neither yours nor mine; divide him between us!" Then the king said, "Do not kill the child, but give him to the woman who wants him to live, for she is his mother!"

(1 Kings 3:16-27 NLT)

Inspiration + Action = Dreams Fulfilled

Fantasia wrote a song entitled "Baby Mama." In that song, she identifies with all the "baby mamas" who struggle to make ends meet, get ahead for themselves and their children, and keep going despite all of life's pressures. She wrote this song to let single mothers know that she understands what they are going through, that she cares about them, and—most importantly—that she knows they can make it if they have a dream and keep going until they see it fulfilled.

Fantasia can say all this authentically through her music because she has been through what single mothers are going through. She, too, has experienced pain and hard times. Oprah Winfrey interviewed her for the September 2007 issue of *O, The Oprah Magazine*. Fantasia shared that she was raped by a ballplayer at school when she was fourteen years old. Other students harassed her so badly, and she had been such a poor student anyhow, that she dropped out of school and moved out of her parents' home into an apartment. With her low sense of self-esteem, she connected with a boy who was not good for her. At seventeen, she became pregnant. Without a diploma or a job, she went on welfare and food stamps.

And yet this poor, young single mother was inspired one night as she watched "American Idol." She put action to her inspiration by borrowing fifty dollars from family members and having her brother drive her to Atlanta for the auditions. After doors miraculously opened that literally had been closed to her, she not only won a spot on the show, but she also became the show's third American Idol. From there, she went on to cut records, appear on TV, make tours, win major awards, and be cast for the coveted role of Celie in the Broadway version of *The Color Purple*. In the midst of all this, she acknowledged that she had challenges with her reading skills but worked to correct that. The road she has traveled since she achieved stardom has not been a smooth one. She has had dark days, has made mistakes, and has not always made wise choices; but she continues to work to make her dreams come true, and she knows that other people can do that as well.

PROPS FOR THE PROSTITUTES

For those of us who have not been in the role of raising children single-handedly, we need a transformation in our thoughts and attitudes about single parents. We need to drop our stereotypes and misjudgments and understand that single parents come in all shapes, sizes, colors, and cultures. They come with varying economic backgrounds and social statuses. They come both as men and women. Not all single parents are alike.

We run across two single parents in 1 Kings 3. Both of these single parents happen to be female prostitutes. Even so, we can learn some principles from these women to help us become better parents. Join me now for a moment of creative storytelling. Let's imagine that these two women came to me together for counseling.

There is one key difference, however, between this "counseling session" and those I have in real life. In actual counseling sessions, I recognize and honor the code of confidentiality. I would *never* say a word about my time spent with anyone in counseling—*never!* I don't preach it, I don't teach it, and I don't try to hint about it on the sly. When someone comes to me for counseling, it is only between that person and me. But these two women from 1 Kings 3 gave me permission to bring you into the counseling session. They want you to hear what we discussed. They want you to hear the dialogue. They want you to know the experiences they had, so they were open and transparent. They want you to learn from what they have already gone through so that it will benefit you.

When these two women came into my office and sat down, the first thing I did was to commend them as parents. To me, counseling is not about putting people down; it is about lifting people up. It is not condemning them, but comforting and strengthening them. I didn't bring them in and start judging them, reproving them, and insulting them. I brought them in to give them insight from the Word of God about the issues that they were facing. This was not about damnation, but about direction. So the first thing I did was to commend them for taking on the responsibility of parenting. I commended them for bringing their babies into this world. They knew that there was a stigma involved with being a single parent. They knew the shame they might face because neither of them knew which man had gotten them pregnant. They had so many men coming and going in their lives and in their bedrooms that neither of them could tell who the fathers of their babies were.

Let me stop and make a point here. The experience of these two women is not the norm for single parents. Most single parents are *not* prostitutes and are *not* sleeping around with one person after another. Actually, the great majority of single parents started out in a loving relationship with a person to whom they were committed. Many were married when they had their children. So, not only are single parents dealing with the responsibility of caring for their children alone, but they are also dealing with the pain of a broken relationship.

But that was not true of these two women because they were prostitutes. They had illicit sexual activity with a variety of men on a regular basis. They could not identify the fathers of their babies. But I still commended them for delivering their babies. They did not abort the blessing of God. I shared with them my belief that life starts at conception, not birth. Psalm 139:13 says, "For you created my inmost being; you knit me together in my mother's womb." And verse 16 says, "Your eyes saw my unformed body; all the days ordained for me were written in your book before one of them came to be." God is with us not just from birth onward, but from the moment that He begins to form us in our mothers' wombs. The Bible teaches us that all children are a blessing from God. And these women chose to allow God's blessings to come into the world through them.

Please know that I am pointing this out only to praise these women and other single parents—not to make any woman feel bad if she has had an abortion at some time in the past. God does not want us to go through life with feelings of guilt. Guilt is designed to bring us to God. Once we have come to God and repented of our sins, we must receive God's forgiveness and restoration. God does not intend for us to drag guilt around with us for the rest of our lives. That does not honor Him and it does not allow us to experience the abundant life that Jesus died to give to us. In Ephesians 1:7-8, we read, "In him we have redemption through his blood, the forgiveness of sins, in accordance with the riches of God's grace that he lavished on us." God's grace is greater than all our sin. There is nothing we have done that God will not forgive. And once He has forgiven us, we need to walk through life with the full assurance of that forgiveness.

But these two prostitutes welcomed their babies. Psalm 127:3-5 tells us that children are a gift from God. Verse 3 puts it like this: "Children are a heritage from the LORD, offspring a reward from him." This biblical blessing is so contrary to the label that is so often given, even to this day, to children who are born out of wedlock. The term "illegitimate" is often still used to label such children. Labeling people is very common because our society follows the unwritten code that says, "If I label you, I can limit you. If I can *de*fine you, I can *con*fine you." But why would anyone want to put a label on a baby? What did that baby do to earn the label "illegitimate"?

All babies are a blessing from God. If you, as a single parent, have come across a pastor or church that says to you, "I won't bless your baby because there is no husband and wife in this situation," you don't have to go home crying about that. It isn't a pastor, minister, or church that determines which babies are blessed. Only God can make that determination, and God says your baby is blessed. When we ministers bless babies, it is merely a ritual to represent what's happening in the spiritual realm. Spiritually, this baby has already been blessed by God. We are just confirming or affirming that the hand of the Lord is upon this child. No matter what your circumstances today, your baby is already blessed.

WILLING TO SACRIFICE, WILLING TO GROW

Another area for which I commended these two women in this counseling session was their wise handling of money. They are single women; they gave birth to babies; the fathers are not there to help them, so all of the financial responsibility for the children falls upon them. These women were smart enough to know that they couldn't afford to take on all of that additional expense in their current situation. Therefore, they decided to move in together and become roommates.

By doing that, these women knew they could cut their expenses in half and have enough to care for their babies as well as themselves. They knew that to stay out of debt, they had to either increase what was coming in or decrease what was going out. They decided to decrease what was going out. In today's world this would mean that instead of the rent being six hundred dollars each, it would only be three hundred. The electric bill was not a hundred and fifty dollars, but seventy-five. They could watch each other's child so they didn't have to incur babysitting costs. All of their expenses were cut in half by moving in together and sharing those expenses.

Now, some women would be opposed to this type of an arrangement because they think that they can't live with anybody. If that's the case, it rules out the possibility of ever being married someday because being married usually means living with somebody. Now, the person who says, "I can't live with anybody" is actually saying, "Nobody can live with me. I don't have enough patience. I am not willing to compromise. I have issues with communicating. I'm not very tolerant and don't want to deal with people who don't think like me, act like me, and do things my way."

Anyone who thinks like that needs to learn to deal with his or her own issues. Being in a committed relationship with someone else, even just as roommates, necessitates change on our part. Learning to be more patient, more thoughtful, more transparent, and more understanding of others are positive changes that we all need to be open to experiencing.

A third thing for which I commended these women was their desire for custody of their children. When you boil this text down to the most fundamental facts, what you have are two parents struggling for custody of one child.

That has to say something to a child—"I have two parents who want me, who want to provide for me, who love me so much that they want me with them." It has to do something for the self-esteem and security of a child to feel so loved and wanted. So I commended these women for the fact that they were embracing their children and embracing motherhood.

ANYTHING FOR THE CHILDREN

Now, in our counseling session, I not only offered commendation to these women for their responses to their children, but I also offered correction to them for some of their illicit practices. When I counsel, I cannot simply say what I think the person wants to hear. I cannot throw out false hopes and dreams and make it seem as though everything is going to work out no matter what the person does. I would be unfaithful to God if I did not incorporate loving correction from the Word of God into the counseling session when the situation calls for that. I would be unfaithful to these women if I simply praised them and sent them on their way with no direction or instruction to take with them. I have the freedom to say to them what I believe they need to hear because *they* came to *me*. They asked me to counsel them. I didn't walk up to them after church some Sunday and say, "Now, this is what I think about your situation . . . ." No, they came to me and asked me for help, so I had to help them as best I knew how—which means sharing with them the principles of God.

The first thing I told them is that their perverted practice of prostitution had to come to an end. I asked them how they could claim to be a parent and a prostitute at the same time. I let them know that they needed to make a choice. They could not be good parents and continue in prostitution. (Remember, they have asked me to share all of this with you.) The answer they gave me regarding their prostitution was, "We will do anything for our children." I asked, "You are saying you would do *anything* for your children?" They responded again, "Yes, that's why we are prostituting. You may want us to stop, but we can't because we have to make money to care for our children, and we would do anything for them." "So, why is it," I asked, "that your willingness to do anything for your children must involve doing something that is harmful to your well-being and theirs, harmful to your health and theirs, and harmful to your future and theirs?" Too often I have heard parents use the supposed welfare of their children to rationalize their own bad behavior: "I steal because I would do anything for my children," "I sell drugs because I would do anything for my children," or "I am a prostitute because I would do anything for my children."

If you are willing to do anything for your children, why not care for them God's way? Why not get your own heart and life right with God? Why not introduce your children to their loving heavenly Father who cares about them? Why not join a good church where you can be nurtured by people who care about you and your children and where your children can be surrounded by other children and adults who are trying to live godly lives? Why not read the Bible to your children so they will better understand who God is? Why not invest in yourself? Why not go back to school and get training or a degree so that you can do something meaningful and rewarding with your life? Why don't you stop demeaning yourself and letting yourself be used and abused? Why not start seeing yourself as God sees you and then let Him take control of your life? If you will do anything for your children, then do something *positive*. That's how I responded to these two women.

Now, we need to also broaden our concept of what prostitution is. Some women would never go out to the streets to sell their bodies to strangers, but they still engage in prostitution. One of the best definitions I have ever heard was offered by the late Dr. John D. Mangram, who served for over twenty years at Bishop College as Dean of the Chapel, Chairman of the Division of Religion and Philosophy, and Professor of Religion. He said, "Prostitution is when you are selling what you are supposed to be giving away out of love." From that definition, we can see that it isn't only women on the streets who are prostitutes.

THE PROSTITUTE AS TEACHER

When talking with these two women, I pointed out that God had blessed them with the gift of sex, but now they were selling it instead of giving it away out of love: "You have this beautiful, amazing gift, but instead you're selling it for rent, a car payment, clothing, or whatever." This holds just as true for a woman who would never go to the streets to prostitute, but responds when a boyfriend calls at 1 a.m. She picks up her smartphone, getting ready to do a dumb thing. The deep, husky voice on the other end says, "It's me. I'm on my way." He comes in under the cloak of darkness, finds the pathetic woman waiting for his sorry behind, does what he wants to do, throws a little money on the nightstand "to help with the rent," and takes off, leaving her like discarded trash. A woman's sexuality, a woman's body, is worth more than that money on the nightstand, more than a car payment, more than any amount of money. It is priceless. It isn't supposed to be sold, but given away out of love.

During the counseling session, I told the women, "You've got to stop prostituting. You've got too many men coming and going. You've got children, and yet you let different men come and go in your home and in your bedroom. I asked, "Do you know what you are teaching your sons and daughters? You are teaching them that this is what relationships look like between men and women. You are teaching them that it is normal for a woman to have multiple sexual partners. You are showing your daughters that it is okay for them to go from one man to the next, giving sexual favors. You are showing your sons that it is okay for them to come in and hit it, quit it, and forget it, with no thought for the feelings of the woman. Your lifestyle is teaching your children louder and more enduring lessons than anything you might say to them with your voice. Even though it is wrong, your behavior becomes their standard for what is right. Is that what you really want to teach your children?"

I called their attention to the fact that their lives were so dysfunctional that they only got with men who got with them for pleasure. They only got with men for financial profit. If there was no profit, they offered no pleasure. Likewise, the men knew that if they were going to get the pleasure, they had to offer the profit. I noted that if that was all their relationships were about, they were always going to have problems because that is unhealthy and dysfunctional. The same man who shows up for pleasure and offers profit is never around when it's time for parenting. Although these women had every right to expect their babies' fathers to accept their responsibility and be there for their children, it should not have taken them by surprise when that did not happen. They knew from the start that these men were only with them for pleasure. They were there for the pleasure, but not for the parenting.

If a woman thinks a self-seeking man who uses her for his own pleasure will suddenly change and feel all fatherly just because he hears that she is pregnant, that isn't likely to happen. If she wants to make sure that she has the life she wants for her and her children, she has to make sure she is making the right decisions at the *beginning* of the relationship. It is at that point that she needs to be asking the man: "Where are you going in life? Do you love me for who I am? What's your relationship with God? Do you already have children, and, if so, are you taking care of them?" These sorts of questions resolved positively at the front end of a relationship will ensure that the woman will not be stalking a man at the back end of the relationship, trying to get what he is unwilling to give.

Happy Dogs, Unhappy Families

These two women had proven that they knew how to get a man, but they didn't know how to keep a man. But they disagreed, saying, "We don't want to keep them. We want them to leave." The reason was that they had given up on marriage. They said they still wanted men, but they didn't want marriage. I had difficulty understanding this. It was God who designed and instituted marriage. Why wouldn't they want to do things God's way? They pointed to the discord in the marriages of their parents, friends, and cousins, as well as the constant stories of contention and divorce in celebrity news. They said they didn't want anything to do with that. They didn't need that kind of fighting, tension, and disappointment in their lives.

But I pointed out to them that they were looking at the wrong examples. Most of their examples were people who married the wrong person for the wrong reason. Indeed, they had not been seeking God's will for their lives. They were certainly not looking for a genuine, selfless, giving love relationship, but rather for someone who would meet their needs. So now these women were skipping the marriage part altogether and simply looking for someone who would meet their needs. Their relationships were somewhat like a relationship with a maintenance man. A maintenance man comes by on occasion to clean the gutters, mow the grass, fix the furnace, or to service whatever needs are there, and then he leaves and goes on to care for somebody else.

Even among the general population today, it is not out of the norm for a couple to live together without being married. They want the benefits of the relationship without the commitment. They want to have their needs met, but to retain their freedom to move on if they feel that this person isn't doing it for them. This is nothing like what God had in mind when He ordained marriage.

In the kind of marriage God ordains, the couple are in the relationship "till death do they part." In the kind of marriage God ordains, the husband loves his wife so much that he lays down his life for her even as Christ lays down His life for the church. He cares more about meeting her needs than his own. In the kind of marriage God ordains, the wife loves and honors her husband—always wanting the best for him, always being his greatest fan.

In a marriage God ordains, God is always at the center of the relationship. The man and woman are both focused on the Lord, wanting to please Him and serve Him. They want Christ to be the Head of their home and they want to reach out together to care for others and to bring others to Jesus. These women in my counseling session, however, wanted to forgo all that God had in store for them in a marriage relationship and continue to see men simply for the men's pleasure and the women's profit.

While talking with these women, I was reminded of Happy, our family dog. My mother brought him home one year as a birthday gift to my sister and brother who are twins. Happy quickly became part of our family, and we all loved the little mutt. His name suited him. He was always active, energetic, spending his time having fun, and he loved to play. I spent a lot of time with Happy. I taught him how to sit, stay, and roll over, and he would do all those things. I taught him to go outside to go to the bathroom and to come back in when he was finished.

We tried to domesticate Happy. But what I discovered was that you can't really domesticate a dog. There was something about Happy's nature that would not change, no matter how many tricks he learned or how much fun we had together. That cute little puppy grew up to be a full-fledged dog. Happy would disappear for hours at a time, and we didn't know where he went.

Eventually, we learned that Happy was having sex with all of the female dogs in the neighborhood. So Mama put up a fence around our yard to try to keep Happy at home. But Happy would jump the fence and be gone for hours, leaving us to wonder and worry about him. But Happy invariably would come back whenever he felt like it. Now, he didn't come back to us because he loved us. He came back because we gave him a place to stay and food to eat. At one point, we even tried putting Happy on a chain; but he broke the chain, ran off, did his thing, and came back when he felt like it.

After this had gone on for a while, all of the female dogs in the neighborhood began having babies, and my friends would invite me over to see their new puppies. I looked at the puppies and instantly recognized the distinctive eyes, noses, and ears, along with the familiar boundless energy and outgoing personality. I knew they all belonged to my dog. Happy was having puppies all over the place, but he never went back to help the mother dogs out with those little ones. He continued on his merry way, doing his own thing, and then leaving the females with all of the responsibility.

I used this story to illustrate to my counselees that there are still a lot of Happy dogs all around us. The women might, somewhere along the line, each meet a Happy dog that makes *them* happy, and they foolishly think that they will be able to domesticate them. This may seem to work for a little while, but then the dogs start leaving for long periods of time. The women have no idea where their dog is going, but they excuse him by saying, "Oh, but he comes back." However, he doesn't come back because he loves you, but rather because you feed him, meet his needs, and give him a place to stay.

KEEP THE LIGHT ON

In addition to talking about the prostitution, I also counseled with these mothers about the harsh reality that their sons were being raised without fathers in their lives. I cautioned them not to smother their sons. One of these women had already done this physically to her son. She held him so close to her that she accidentally rolled over on him and suffocated him. She then took her dead son, exchanged his body for the other woman's live son, and took the living baby to her own bed, acting as though nothing had happened.

When the other woman picked up her son the next morning to nurse him, she realized the baby was not breathing. She cried out that her son was dead, but then, in the light of the morning, she saw that this baby was not her son at all. He belonged to the other woman who had kidnapped *her* son, acting as though he belonged to her.

It took light for this woman to see that the dead child wasn't hers and recognize that her own child was alive. When we look at our own children in the light of God's Word and by the Light of Jesus—even if we thought they were as good as dead and that there was no hope—we will see that there is still life in them.

We have to stop looking for life in the dark. When we look around and can see only gloom and doom, darkness and depression, we cannot see the life that is there. We assume our situation is dead. But when we shed the Light of God on the situation (through our relationship with Jesus and God's Word), the Light reveals that it is not dead after all. It is still alive and there is still hope.

We also need to keep the Light shining in our children's lives. The Light of Jesus should shine on what our children see, what they hear, where they go, and with whom they spend their time. A mixed-up situation at a Brooklyn hospital illustrates this point. Two women went to the hospital during the same time period to give birth to their babies. The women had the same last name, and the first letter of their first names was also the same. After delivering her baby, one of the women had some physical issues that required further surgery and care, so it was two days before she was able to see her new baby. During that time, the hospital mistakenly confused her baby with the other woman's baby, and the other woman had already begun nursing and bonding with that child.

By the time the woman had recovered from her surgery, the hospital had corrected their error and brought her the right baby. But the baby would not nurse from her. The baby would not receive from her own mother because she had tasted another's milk first.

This illustrates why we have to be careful not to let our children taste the things of the world. We want to offer them love, nurturing, and guidance, but if they have tasted what the world is offering, they may not be satisfied with what we are giving them. We need to know what movies they watch and what music they listen to, along with what videos they watch and what else they view on websites. And we have to evaluate all those things in the Light of God's Word. Otherwise, when we come to them saying (as it does in Psalm 34:8), "Taste and see that the Lord is good," they may refuse to taste, and want what is unhealthy for them because they are used to that other taste. We have to keep the Light on!

DON'T SUFFOCATE YOUR CHILD!

It may seem easy to judge the mother who suffocated her child and then tried to take someone else's child to replace her own. But my heart goes out to her. My heart goes out to any parent who loses a child in death. No parents should have to bury their own child. My heart also goes out to any parent whose child is still alive yet lost, even as the prodigal son in Jesus' parable was lost.

My heart goes out to any parent who has lost a child to drugs, alcohol, gangs, violence, pornography, ignorance, or incarceration. But I know that we serve a God of restoration, renewal, and revival. I know that Jesus can even raise up dead situations. Even as the father in the story of the prodigal son said, "For this son of mine was dead and is alive again; he was lost and is found" (Luke 15:24), so do parents today rejoice as they see God bring their own children back to life.

But this woman whose own son died told me in our counseling session that she wanted me to pass along a warning to other single parents, and especially to single mothers raising sons. She said emphatically, "Don't suffocate your child!" She admitted that she held her son too close, and eventually he couldn't breathe. With great sorrow, she said, "My son never had a chance in life to grow up to be a man because he stayed too close to me for too long."

Of course, some women respond to this counsel by saying of their sons, "But I am both his mama and daddy." I know what that means. I understand where they are coming from. They mean that they have to do it all. In addition to all of the things that they think a mother would naturally do, they have to do whatever they consider the role of the father to be as well. When my wife and I had our first child, we took turns. She didn't have to change every diaper, and I didn't have to feed our son every time he was hungry. We took turns caring for his needs. But a single parent doesn't have that option. Whatever has to be done, it is on his or her shoulders to do it. There is no trading off. So I do understand what single parents mean when they say that they must be both mother and father to their children.

It is crucial, however, for single mothers with sons to understand that they can give the message of manhood to a boy, but they cannot become the model of manhood. A single mother can offer her son the principles of manhood, but she is not a prototype of what it means to be a man. If a man is ever going to grow psychologically from boyhood to manhood, he has to see what a real man looks like. The only way he can become a man is by learning from a real man. No matter how much a woman can *tell* him about manhood, she can never *show* that to him. She needs to work together with the boy's grandfather, uncle, coach, neighbor, or Big Brother—someone who can serve as his positive role model for being a man.

I always encourage men to serve as a role model for at least one boy or young man in their lives. If we made it effectively from boyhood to manhood, we need to reach back and help another young man along. God cared for us along the way so that we can care for others. We need to let little boys and young men know from our lives that real men love Jesus, real men participate at church and in the community, real men take care of their families, real men are loving toward their wives, and real men work for a living. They need to *see* a real man before they know how to *be* a real man.

KNOW WHEN TO LET GO

But some women think they can do it all themselves. As a result, they smother their sons. They end up doing too much for too long for their sons until their sons don't learn to do things for themselves. We see men all around us with arrested development. At a time when they should be mature, accepting responsibility, and growing into the persons God created them to be, they are still childish, irresponsible, and letting their mothers take care of them.

At some point, a mother has to stop giving her son a bath and let him bathe himself. At some point, he has to learn to pick out clothes and put them on himself. At some point, he has to learn to go to school without his mother taking him there by the hand. At some point, he must learn to speak up for himself and not turn to his mother when someone asks him a question. At some point, he has to learn to pick up after himself and clean up his own messes. At some point, he needs to learn how to cook for himself, do his own laundry, make his own bed, care for his own room, and do chores around the house. At some point, he has to learn to drive on his own. He has to go on dates without his mother in the backseat. He has to go off to college and make the grades for himself. He has to get a job without his mama sitting in on the interview. If he is ever going to become a man, he has to come out from under his mother's wings.

If a woman refuses to step aside and let that happen, she will forever have this dependent, immature male son who wants to stay in her home, eat her food, watch her television all day, take her money, let her wait on him hand and foot, and never feel that there is anything wrong with that picture. He won't be worthy of a good woman or a good job. But she thought she could do it all herself and she didn't want to let go.

It is just as true that a single dad needs to make sure that his daughter has a female role model. She needs to learn what a real woman looks like, as well as how she thinks and acts. She will be bombarded with all kinds of celebrity images telling her what she should do, what make-up to wear, how she should dress, and the way she should think about boys and love. Her daddy can and certainly should give input into her life about such matters, but he can't *model* for her what it means to be a woman or talk to her from a female perspective.

A girl needs a grandmother, aunt, teacher, or Big Sister—someone who loves God and can model for her what it means to be a godly woman. She needs to hear a woman who loves God pray, see how a Christian woman cares for her family, and learn how godly women have made decisions about what to do with their lives. She needs a woman to talk to, especially as she gets older and her body starts to develop from that of a child into a young woman.

Daddy can't tell her as she grows older how it feels to be touched by a man and how her body will respond. He can't talk with her about how it feels to have PMS. He can't explain to her why she will still likely want to have babies when she grows up, in spite of all the pain of childbirth that she has seen on some TV show. A daughter needs a loving woman alongside her when it's time to buy her first bra, when she has just started her first period, and when she thinks she has fallen in love.

A man doesn't think like a woman, so he can't possibly explain certain things in a way that a young woman will understand them or be able to relate. If a man thinks he can do that and insists on playing the "mommy" role throughout his daughter's life, he will likely cause a lot of frustration for his daughter, along with tension between the two of them.

In addition, if Daddy isn't careful, he can easily end up spoiling his "little girl" to the point that no man will ever be able to please her. It's sweet when daddies and their little girls are close and they talk together and do things together. But some fathers learn early on that giving her presents makes his little girl happy. She hugs him and says he's "the best daddy in the whole world," which makes him feel good and feeds his ego. As time goes on, the presents get bigger, and the little girl gets used to telling Daddy everything she wants because he wants to keep her happy. If she is used to getting everything she wants, most young men just starting out in life cannot satisfy those demands, and most *good* men of any age would not *want* a wife who is selfish, demanding, and materialistic. Daddy may be spoiling her for a genuine, loving relationship in the future.

A father needs to learn to gradually let go of his daughter so that she can be free to be the woman God created her to be. If there is no other woman in his life, it may be harder for him to do that. He needs to recognize that giving her things does not obligate her to lifelong dependency. And if he truly loves his daughter and the relationship is healthy, he will not want that from her anyway.

DON'T SETTLE

While talking with the woman who lost her baby, I observed that, without realizing it, she had become dependent on him—the "man" who was always there for her, the man who would always love her, the man who needed her. Caring for him became her identity, made her feel she had purpose in her life, and rewarded her with a dependency that she mistook for love.

In fact, one of the points of counsel I offered to these women was that they must not put a boy in their lives where they used to put a man. This baby should not have been in his mother's bed. She was used to having a man there, but she had her baby there instead. Some women get to the point that they are willing to let someone come into their bed who is less than a man, as they would define true manhood.

Let's say a Christian woman knows that a single Christian man has five essentials in his life: 1) he has accepted Jesus Christ as his Lord and Savior and has direction for his life; 2) he seeks God daily in prayer and Bible study; 3) he is active in his church and in some positive way in his community; 4) he honors the sanctity of sex and wants to marry a godly woman; and 5) he is responsible enough to be earning a living, tithing, and using his money wisely. Now, most women have a few other "must-haves" that they would add to their list (a sense of humor, for example), but let's say that these are the essential basics.

But some women are not willing to wait for a man like this to come along. They have tried Singles.com; Meet Someone New at Lunch.com; Meet Your Mate.com, and every dot-com you can think of, but they just haven't found the right person. So now, instead of waiting for a real man to come along, they lower their standards. They may rationalize, "Well, he *says* he goes to church"; "Well, if that teacher hadn't been so rough on him, he would have finished school"; "Well, I can't blame him for quitting that job because that boss sounds terrible"; "Well, I've heard that he has two or three children by other women, but I just don't believe it"; or "Well, I don't really like the way he treats me, but it'll get better." And they knowingly accept less than a man into their bed.

But one day, they are going to roll over and need some support, but it won't be there. They are going to roll over and need a strong arm to hold them, but it won't be there. They are going to roll over seeking real love, but it won't be there. Someone who is still a boy cannot offer what real men offer.

Take It to the King

My final challenge to these women in our counseling session was, "Take your issues to the King." I told them that I was happy that they had come to me, seeking support from a pastor. I praised them for seeking out new insights from a man of God based on the Word of God. I explained to them that even though I have God's heart for them as a pastor, the gift of encouragement to offer them hope, and the Word of God that I can expound upon for them as a pastor/teacher, their issues go beyond what a pastor, counselor, or teacher can do for them. It's good for them to get all they can from such professionals who are trained to help and can offer words of wisdom, insight, and revelation. But seeing them alone is not enough. These women still need to talk to the King for themselves.

I encouraged them that they have direct access to the King. Despite their illicit relationships, sexual promiscuity, and lifestyle outside the will of God, they still have access to the King. I told them not to let anyone tell them otherwise. I told them that they could never mess up so badly that the King would refuse to see them. Jesus is Lord of lords and King of kings. No matter what we've done in the past, we can still go to Jesus.

When Jesus died on the cross, the veil in the temple was torn in two, from top to bottom. That was God's way of saying that we can have direct access to Him. We don't need an earthly high priest to go for us into the holy place. Jesus is always there to receive us. Ephesians 3:12 says, "In him and through faith in him we may approach God with freedom and confidence." I assured these women that even though they have already talked with so many people about their issues, the King is the One who can really help them. The King can do what nobody else can do.

"Cut the Child in Two!"

So the two women in 1 Kings 3 went to the king and began to argue. The woman whose baby had been taken explained what had happened. She told how the other woman had stolen her baby after unintentionally suffocating her own baby. She told the king, "The live baby is mine." But the other woman insisted, "No! The live baby is mine!" They kept arguing until the king stopped them by saying, "Bring me a sword" (1 Kings 3:24).

When the sword was brought to the king, he ordered the living child to be cut in two so that each woman could have half. Now, if we were looking at this command on the surface, we would be horrified by what the king ordered. We would wonder about his character and values, and how he could possibly make such an outrageous order. But the king knew what he was doing. He was making a point to the women: "If you are going to keep trying to divide this child psychologically and emotionally by pulling him one way and then another, you might as well just tear him apart physically as well. What you are doing is just as harmful as physically tearing him in two."

This is applicable today for situations in which squabbling parents are pulling their child one way and then another. When the eight-year-old child is with her mother, the mother is telling her that her daddy is no good, doesn't pay support, and doesn't really love her. Then, when she's with her daddy, she hears that her mother is no good, doesn't do what she is supposed to, and doesn't really love her. The child is constantly pulled one way and then another, psychologically and emotionally. She doesn't know whom to believe. She doesn't know if either parent really cares about her. At a time when she needs security, peace, and love, her parents are creating havoc in her world, her mind, and her heart. The child cannot be whole because the parents keep pulling her apart.

Often what happens is that the parents take their argument to a court of law and one of them rejoices over getting full custody of the child. While that parent is so happy and feels good about "winning," the other parent is despondent and heartbroken. But more than that, we have to wonder how much the child is losing in that process. Will the child grow up without the nurturing intimacy of a mother's love or without the strong sense of security and protection she feels when she is with her father? No matter how the parents feel about each other or the outcome of the battle, the child has always lost a part of himself or herself. Part of the child is destroyed.

So the wise King Solomon didn't go that route. He didn't tell one mother or the other to take the child. Instead, he ordered that the baby be cut in two with a sword and half be given to each mother. He already knew that the real mother of the baby, the woman who truly loved this child, would not allow her baby to be destroyed like that. Instead, she selflessly said, "Don't kill the baby. Let her have the child. I would rather see him live a whole life than to be destroyed by being divided between us."

KING JESUS CHANGES THE GAME

We have a greater King among us than Solomon. King Jesus knows how to work out the difficulties of our lives. When parents are at war with each other, King Jesus understands the father and understands the mother, but He is really on the side of the child. When His disciples were trying to keep a group of children from "bothering" Jesus, Jesus said to them, "Let the little children come to me, and do not hinder them, for the kingdom of heaven belongs to such as these" (Matthew 19:14).

God has a place in His heart for children. In Genesis 21, when Hagar had given her son, Ishmael, the last of the water Abraham had given her before sending the two of them off into the desert, verse 16 tells us she separated herself from her son because she didn't want him to die and "she began to sob." But it was not *her* cries, but the cries of the child Ishmael that got the attention of God. Verse 17 says, "God heard the boy crying," and the angel of God called out to Hagar and told her what to do to save herself and the boy.

Even in heaven, God has a place in His heart for children. When King David tragically lost the first baby he had with his beloved Bathsheba, he began to look forward with hope to the day that they would be reunited. In 2 Samuel 12:23, he made the point that even though his son could not come back here to him, he knew that he could one day go to his son. He knew that his child was safe with

God. Whether they are on this earth or in heaven, God always has a place in His heart for children.

When I was growing up, we didn't have all the technological games that children play with today. We used to play board games a lot, including Monopoly, Life, chess, and checkers. I was great at chess, but horrible at checkers. I did well at chess because I knew there was a strategy and I could analyze the strategy. For the longest time, with checkers, I just thought you were moving and jumping, moving and jumping. I didn't realize there was any strategy involved. My two brothers loved to play that game with me because they would always win. My sister used to talk me into playing it with her because she knew she was going to win. I was terrible.

One thing I did learn about checkers, however, was that if I could get one of my pieces—even just one—to king's row, that was going to change the nature of the game. After I had made it to king's row, I could move in ways that I couldn't move before, operate in ways I couldn't operate before, and maneuver in ways I couldn't maneuver before.

In our lives, if we can make it to the King, that changes the nature of the game. No matter how bad things have been, once we get to King Jesus, everything changes. No matter how much we've gone through and how many defeats we've experienced, King Jesus can turn things around. There is power in King Jesus; healing in King Jesus; comfort in King Jesus; and inspiration in King Jesus. King Jesus can resolve all of our issues and bring victory into our lives.

King Jesus,

We are so grateful today that we can come to You and know assuredly that we are welcome. We are sorry for our sins and the many times that we fail You, not only as parents but in all walks of life. Forgive us, Lord, and empower us so that each today will be better than yesterday, and each tomorrow better than today. Let us continually grow to be more and more like You. You know the many problems and issues that are on our heart this day. Thank You that there is nothing too big for You to handle. No problem frightens You, and no issue overwhelms You. Grant us wisdom to know what to do in our lives, and grace to enable us to do that. Comfort us in all of our losses, for the pain is deep. Touch our eyes that we might better see You. Touch our ears that we might better hear Your voice. Give us hope for tomorrow. Delight us with Your Presence and help us to experience Your love afresh and anew. Amen.

CHAPTER 3

THE FAITH FACTOR
OF THE SINGLE PARENT

Some time later the brook dried up because there had been no rain in the land. Then the word of the LORD came to him: "Go at once to Zarephath in the region of Sidon and stay there. I have directed a widow there to supply you with food." So he went to Zarephath. When he came to the town gate, a widow was there gathering sticks. He called to her and asked, "Would you bring me a little water in a jar so I may have a drink?" As she was going to get it, he called, "And bring me, please, a piece of bread."

"As surely as the LORD your God lives," she replied, "I don't have any bread—only a handful of flour in a jar and a little olive oil in a jug. I am gathering a few sticks to take home and make a meal for myself and my son, that we may eat it—and die."

Elijah said to her, "Don't be afraid. Go home and do as you have said. But first make a small loaf of bread for me from what you have and bring it to me, and then make something for yourself and your son. For this is what the LORD, the God of Israel, says: 'The jar of flour will not be used up and the jug of oil will not run dry until the day the LORD sends rain on the land.'"

She went away and did as Elijah had told her. So there
was food every day for Elijah and for the woman and her
family. For the jar of flour was not used up and the jug of
oil did not run dry, in keeping with the word of the LORD
spoken by Elijah.

(1 Kings 17:7-16)

WHEN THE LOVE DIES

This book continually stresses that we reject the negative ste-
reotype of the single parent and that we are not condemning single
parents, but rather coming alongside to comfort and strengthen
them. We are moving beyond the myth that all single parents have
engaged in a series of illicit sexual affairs. According to the latest
data from the U.S. census, most single parents come from loving,
committed relationships that went awry, leaving them to care for
their children alone.

We know that fifty percent of first marriages in America end
in divorce. Seventy percent of second marriages end in divorce.
Seventy-four percent of third marriages end in divorce. It serves
us no purpose in this book to discuss all of the reasons for these
high rates of divorce. The reality, however, is that when these marriages end, it often results in someone becoming a single parent. The
person of the opposite sex who was previously readily available to
each of them is no longer there.

It is important to understand this new reality of the single parent.
He or she was used to having someone alongside. This person probably provided companionship; made possible an ongoing intimate
and loving sexual relationship; shared in household responsibilities;
helped nurture, love, and discipline the children; afforded a greater
sense of security; provided the opportunity for satisfying adult conversation; and shared in providing financially for the family. Imagine
all of that suddenly being taken away.

When God created us, He made us physical beings (forming
us from the dust of the earth); and He made us spiritual beings
(breathing into us the breath of life); and He made us sexual beings
(enabling us to be fruitful and multiply). We have to acknowledge

all aspects of our personhood. Just because we are spiritual beings does not make us any less physical or sexual. We are made with those three aspects, and they are all beautiful in God's sight.

In Genesis 1, we read that whenever God completed a new creation, He saw that "it was good." The light, the land and seas, the plants and trees, the sun and moon, the birds and sea life, the livestock and wild animals—all of this, God said, was "good." But after He created human beings, after He created *us*, He said it was "*very* good."

No matter how strong a Christian or how spiritual a saint we are, we are still also physical and sexual. In fact, I think that the more spiritual we become, the more sexual we become. (Maybe I am speaking only from my own experience, but I do believe that is true.) The more we exercise our bodies, the healthier we become overall. The more we exercise our minds and our spirits, the healthier we become overall. So it only stands to reason that the more we exercise ourselves sexually, the healthier we become overall. Now, of course, everything can be carried to an extreme or done in an unhealthy way. For instance, engaging in too much physical exertion while getting too little water and food is unhealthy. Using our minds and spirits to focus on the occult, violence in movies or video games, or only the negative things in life are all unhealthy. In the same way, engaging in sex selfishly, out of wedlock, or in an addictive manner are all unhealthy as well.

But think about the person who has had a healthy sexual relationship within a loving marriage. But then the marriage ends abruptly. One of the partners was expecting this to last "till death do us part." But now it's over. The person who was used to having sex five times a week or twice a week, or whatever worked for that couple, is now alone. Does that person miss the sex? Absolutely! Unless there was something perverted or unhealthy in the way sex was experienced in that relationship, the person is left feeling that part of his or her being is now totally dormant. It may still demand attention, but there is no loving sexual engagement to satisfy the need.

LET'S KEEP IT REAL

Now, some people really perplex me. They try to be so holy that they say they don't need fulfillment in this area of their lives. Some will say, "Oh, since I've become a Christian, I just don't think of sex like I used to." Or, "I'm going through a season in my life in which I am focused on my spiritual life and I just have no desire for sex." They sound so sanctimonious, so self-righteous. There is nothing attractive in that type of attitude, and it doesn't ever ring true.

It reminds me of the story of Mother Sadie, a middle-aged woman who taught little children in Sunday school. She never missed a Sunday. She would have the little children sitting on the floor, gathered around her, as she shared with them the Sunday school lesson every Sunday. Her common refrain to the children was, "Mama Sadie doesn't need anybody but Jesus. For Mama Sadie, it's just me and Jesus and nobody else. Jesus is all Mama Sadie ever needs." Every Sunday, it was the same thing: "Mama Sadie doesn't need anybody but Jesus. Jesus is all Mama Sadie ever needs." This went on Sunday after Sunday as part of each lesson she taught.

Then one Sunday, the children went by Mama Sadie's house early on their way to Sunday school. As they walked by, they saw a man climb out of her window and run through the back yard with his shirt open and shoes in his hand. They went on to Sunday school, sat down on the floor as usual, and Mama Sadie took her place in the chair. As she began to teach her usual weekly lesson, one of the little boys raised his hand and said, "Mama Sadie, we saw Jesus coming out of your house this morning with His shoes in His hands!" We are sexual beings, too.

GRIEVING TAKES TIME

It takes time for individuals to get over a long-term relationship. The amount of time depends on many factors. How long was the relationship? What was the level of commitment in the relationship? (Married? Living together? Dating?) Are children involved? How intertwined have their lives become? (Do their families get together often? Are most of their friends mutual? Do they engage in the same pastimes?) How satisfying and rewarding was the relationship? What caused the break-up? What does the financial situation look like? There are some spouses who cannot even remember when their ex-partner's birthday is, yet there are others who break out in tears every time they see the other person's favorite color. There are so many factors that determine how long it will be before someone can move on after a serious relationship. But it is likely that the time will be measured in years, as opposed to weeks or months.

This is especially true when the couple has been married. God says that in marriage, two become one. Divorce tears that one apart. The partners don't simply divide back into the same two entities they were before the marriage. They have each become a part of the other. They don't simply go back to being two "single" people. They are one person who is torn in two. We need to expect that one may feel that his or her heart has been torn out. We need to recognize that there will be wounds, rough edges, and bare places that need time to heal. We need to be patient while divorced people work to put themselves back together again so that they can function as a whole, as they once were. Separating physically takes only seconds; it's as simple as one person walking away. But the psychological, emotional, and spiritual connections remain.

We may let a partner go physically, but that person stays in our spirit for a very long time. This is why subsequent marriages are often doomed from the start. When someone marries another person while that first person is still in his or her spirit, there really isn't room for the new person in that relationship. When we are psychologically and emotionally still tied to someone from our past, we don't need to keep trying to connect with someone new.

GOD WORKS BEHIND THE SCENES

In 1 Kings 17, we find that God is developing this man Elijah as His man and calling him to be a prophet. God is also working in the life of a widow who lives in Zarephath. God is directing her. We know this because the Lord tells Elijah, "I have directed a widow there to supply you with food" (v. 9). God is operating in this situation, and He is at work in both of their lives.

This is a time of drought. Verse 1 says that the prophet Elijah is sent to King Ahab, the most evil of all the kings that Israel ever had. He tells Ahab that God will not allow it to rain in that area for the next few years. This meant there would be an economic downturn. Everything alive is dependent on water, but there would be no water for years in this area. The effect of the drought would be catastrophic.

The widow in this story lives in an area called Sidon, named after one of Noah's descendants. Noah had a son named Ham, Ham had a son named Canaan, and Canaan had a son named Sidon. Africans and their ancestors originated from the lineage of Ham. The Jews came from the lineage of Noah's son Shem, while Europeans traced their roots back to his son Japheth.

The genealogical breakdown after the flood can be found in Genesis 10, which some theologians refer to as the Table of Nations. It is interesting when we realize that only Noah and his family survived the flood. That means that everyone on the face of the earth today can be traced back ultimately to Noah, which means that we are all related. And yet, racism somehow continues to find acceptance in hearts and minds today. It doesn't make sense.

But I share that detail about our genealogy simply to point out that this woman from Sidon is a person of color. We also learn from the Scriptures that she is a widow, so we know that her husband has died. And we know that this widow has a son whom she is raising alone, so she also is a single parent. Along with all of the others in her region, she is experiencing a drought, so everything has dried up. There is no rain for the crops and no water to keep the animals alive. Everything in that area is dying.

However, when we first encounter this woman, she isn't lying at home bemoaning their depleted assets. Nor is she angry with God. She isn't asking, "God, how can You allow me to have lost everything just because Ahab is being punished for the evil he has done? This situation isn't my fault, and I have a child to raise. Why would You do this?" Instead, she is out in the field working, gathering sticks, so that she can at least put to use their limited resources. She is feeling hopeless, but she's still doing what she can do. She has only a handful of flour and a little olive oil left. Her plan is to take the sticks home to start a fire. Then she will make a tiny loaf of bread that she and her son will eat before they die.

Notice that God is using this drought to *discipline* Ahab. He is using the same drought to *develop* Elijah. And he is using the very same drought to *direct* the widow. The drought is one event, but God is doing three different things with it.

SAME CIRCUMSTANCE, MULTIPLE PURPOSES

Some women in the widow's position would have been upset with God for allowing someone else's behavior to bring about a negative situation for *them*. But God would have responded, "I am not using the drought to discipline you, only to direct you." If Elijah had questioned God, God would have said to him, "I am not using the drought to discipline you, only to develop you." When we look at circumstances, especially negative ones caused by someone else's behavior, we can be tempted to feel that God is being unfair in letting those things happen to us. But if we could look at the situation from God's perspective, we would see that while we are sharing a circumstance with others, God is using it differently in our lives than He is in theirs. We need to learn to trust God in the midst of our droughts.

Young preachers frequently ask me how I approach a text for a sermon or lesson. I tell them that I boil the text down to its most basic fundamental elements and then I am able to see and understand it a whole lot better. When I boiled down 1 Kings 17 to its most basic fundamental elements, what I saw was that God was developing a man. God knew that this was the man who would stand against the wicked Ahab and the evil Jezebel. This was the man who would challenge almost a thousand false prophets. This was the man who needed to hear God in a whisper. This was the man who would mentor the great prophet Elisha. This was the man who would one day enter into heaven in a whirlwind. God knew all that Elijah would face in his life, so He used this hard season of drought to develop him and prepare him for the things he had to do in the days ahead.

So God was developing a man; God was directing a woman; and it was already in God's plan to bring them together for a holy hookup. Now, theirs was not a romantic hookup, but if God could bring these two unlikely people together for His purposes, He certainly can also bring together a man and a woman for a loving life-long relationship.

People sometimes ask me what I think of online dating and Internet matchmaking. It really doesn't matter what I think. That is part of our culture today. For whatever reason, today when men or women want to go out, instead of approaching a friend or acquaintance, they go online to find someone they've never heard of, never seen before, and don't know anything about. Then they go out on a date together without any sense of accountability. Their family and friends don't know the person; in fact, nobody they know knows the person. Yet they go out anyway, trusting that the person is who he or she claims to be. Apparently they expect that person to be a better possibility than all of the people they know from work, all of the people they know at school, all of the people they know from church, and all of the people they know through friends and family.

I know that people sometimes find a match that way, but I still believe that God is the greatest Matchmaker of all. I still believe that God does cosmic connections. I believe that God knows how to make a holy hookup. God knows how to take a God-developed man and hook him up with a God-directed woman in order to accomplish His purposes. God works on both ends at the same time. But it takes faith to know that this happens.

On one end, God was working on this single mother in Sidon who was God-directed. At the other end, he was working on a man who was God-developed. Then God navigated the circumstances of life to put them together in the same place at the same time in order to get their cosmic connection. God is the one who made that happen.

GOD WORKS FROM THE BEGINNING AND THE END

But all this takes faith because we can't see our end. We can see what God is doing with us, but we can't see the other end. We can't see what God is doing with the other person. So, we have to have enough faith to know that while God is working with us on one end, He is also working on the person we need at the other end. So we live by what we know and see, and trust God for what we don't know and see.

In 2006 the Indianapolis Colts won the Super Bowl. Tony Dungy was the coach. When the team won the Super Bowl, everyone was talking about Peyton Manning. Of course, Peyton Manning is the greatest quarterback who ever lived, so there was reason for people to talk about him. But it wasn't only about Peyton Manning. That was also the time the Colts had Dwight Freeney (with double-digit sacks) playing left end and Robert Mathis (with double-digit sacks) the right end. With Freeney at one end and Mathis at the other, they got the ultimate victory because they worked both ends at the same time. In the same way, God is working a victory in our lives because He can work both ends at the same time.

People are debating about whether or not LeBron James will be considered one of the best basketball players who ever lived. The very fact that people are talking about him along with Oscar Robertson, Michael Jordan, Wilt Chamberlain, and Bill Russell means that he is at least on the way to becoming one of the greatest. But he is not one of the greatest players just because he can shoot three-pointers, dunk the ball, make passes, and get assists. That's at the offensive end. He is one of the greatest because he can also guard a point guard, a center, or anyone in between down at the defensive end. He will be one of the greatest players because he works both ends at the same time.

One of the members of my church recently walked up to me and said, "Pastor, we just sold our company." He had been operating a major company in New York City. He went on to explain, "Our executive team came together because someone made us this amazing offer that we just could not refuse. It was so much money that we just couldn't turn it down. So Pastor, I worked my way out of a job. I was the lead on the sale of the company, the one who negotiated the contract, and I made it happen. I told my wife that I was going to come home and be a househusband." He continued to tell me, however, that there was something that he didn't know. He said, "While I was working a good deal for us at the sellers' end, what I didn't know was that the buyers had their eyes on me. When the sale went through, they called and told me that they wanted me to run their company." What he didn't know was that God was working both ends at the same time.

In John 14:3, Jesus said, "And if I go and prepare a place for you, I will come back and take you to be with me that you also may be where I am." Jesus is working both ends at the same time. He is preparing a place for us, and He is also preparing us for the place. His admonition to us would be, "But if you don't let Me prepare you for the place, you won't be ready for the place when the place gets ready for you." But if we allow God to work on us and in us, He can then position us at the right time to receive what He has for us. He is working both ends at the same time.

Trust God During the Process

If you are reading this book as a single person, God would encourage you to be sure that you are letting Him develop and direct you so that He can bring you together with the person whom He is also developing and directing. If you are too busy doing your own thing in your own way, you will miss the opportunity when it's time for God to make it happen. If you are a man and want a God-directed woman in your life, you need to let God develop you as a man. This is important because God-directed women do not want undeveloped men. If you are a woman and want a God-developed man—one who loves Jesus, participates in church, cares for the poor, has a good work ethic, and knows how to treat a wife and children—then you need to let God direct you. This is important because God-developed men do not want misdirected women.

In the 1 Kings 17 story, God had been developing Elijah and directing the widow of Sidon. The first person Elijah saw when he got to Zarephath was this very woman. She was in the right place, and now it was the right time. Notice that while the Bible says that God directed her, there is no verse that says God actually spoke to her. God spoke to the man, but in this passage, He did not speak to this woman. Yet the verse says that God directed her. You may be wondering how that could work. How can God direct a person without talking to him or her? We have to remember that God will often work through circumstances to get us into the right place at the right time.

God didn't say anything to this woman, but He allowed her to be in her current situation. He allowed her to be a single mother raising a child. He allowed her resources to be depleted. But at the same time, He allowed her to keep going even when she felt helpless. Although she had just one last little loaf of bread that she could make, she busied herself doing just that instead of giving up. So when Elijah found her, she was picking up sticks to start the fire to make her bread. She wasn't on the streets trying to pick up a man to care for her or rescue her in exchange for what he might want from her. When a woman has the heavenly Father, she doesn't have to step outside His will to find a sugar daddy to pay the bills. This woman would rather pick up sticks than pick up something outside the will of God.

One thing I am trying to stress with my adult sons right now is the concept of timing. They always want to talk about the right woman and whether or not they have found the right woman, but they aren't eager to ask themselves if this is the right time. Don't misunderstand me; I get excited about marriage. I have such a great marriage that I want that for everyone, especially my own sons. Marriage is sacred and instituted by God. I have no issues about my sons getting married, but I do question them about whether this is the right time for them to consider entering into that lifelong relationship.

One way a man can know whether it's the right time for marriage is that his interest in other women will diminish. If a man is considering proposing to one woman but is still thinking about what it would be like to date another woman whom he sees at church, how he might be able to connect with yet another woman with whom he works, or how he wishes he could be with his new neighbor who just moved next door, it *isn't* the right time.

Another way a man will know it's the right time for marriage is that he will be able to support himself as well as a family. If he still has his hand in Daddy's pocket or Mother's purse, it isn't the right time. In the same way, a couple can know it is the right time to have a baby—not just by their mutual desire to have one, but if they have the means to support one. Timing truly is everything.

NOT EVERY MEETING IS MEANT FOR MARRIAGE

One other element is critical. Single people must recognize that when God brings a man and a woman together, He does it for a purpose. God had a specific purpose in mind for bringing Elijah and the widow together. A man and woman have to meet for the same reason that God wants them to meet. A single mother feeling the huge responsibility of caring for a child especially needs to guard against any attempt on her part to change the purpose for the meeting.

When God brought Elijah and this single mother together, the purpose was for her to feed him. This initial meeting was only about her preparing a meal for the prophet. When God brings a man and woman together for a meal, the woman must be careful not to turn the meeting into an interview for a marriage. Sometimes, it's just a meal. Not every man is a candidate for marriage. God sends some men along simply to be friends. There is a season and a reason for the meeting. When the season is over and the reason has been accomplished, the woman shouldn't get mad at the man because their meeting didn't lead to marriage. That was not God's intention. It may have become her wish, but it was not what God had in mind in bringing them together.

When a man asks a woman out to dinner, usually it means only that he would like to have her company over dinner. Yet some women have a way of jumping ahead and letting their fantasies run away with them, especially if they have not had much male attention recently, and especially if they have been praying to God for a husband. So the poor man who asks out such a woman may find himself the object of much more than he intended. She is so convinced that this is *the* man that they begin as friends during the appetizer, but she is envisioning their wedding day by dessert.

She may even make the conversation very uncomfortable. "What do you think about marriage?" she asks eagerly.

"Well, I think marriage is great. My parents have a good marriage. I imagine I'll get married someday."

"When do you think you will get married? Do you think it will happen soon?"

"My dad told me not even to think about getting married until I'm thirty, so I've got two more years before I even think about it," he replies, shifting uncomfortably in his seat.

Then she peppers him with questions such as these: "Yes, but do you think you will be getting married early or late? How many kids do you want to have? Where do you want to have your wedding? How many groomsmen do you think you will have? Who's going to be your best man? Do you think you'll let your pastor do the wedding?" And on she goes, totally oblivious to his nonverbal cues indicating that he has already decided he will never be seeing her again.

The meeting was just for a meal. That's all he had in mind and all that he asked of her. In fact, now he can hardly wait for this meal to end. Then this clueless woman gets angry later on because this man hasn't called her back. She complains, "No man wants to go out with a woman who has a child." But that's not the reason. No man wants to go out with a woman who has a *chain*. It isn't the child; it's the chain that's scaring men away. They don't want to think of themselves on lockdown when they aren't even ready for marriage.

Not every man God brings into a woman's life is meant for marriage. There is a reason and a season for the encounter. Sometimes it's just for friendship. God knows that most of us enjoy being around the opposite sex. He knows that the woman invited to dinner had been in a bad relationship that ended up broken. Maybe He wants to let her see that not all men are like that one who walked away from her and her baby. Maybe God wants to bless her with a male friend because it would be healthy for her to hear a male viewpoint once in a while. Maybe God just knows that she is lonely and needs a male friend. Whatever God's purpose in bringing the two together, chances are it is not for marriage. So she needs to relax, enjoy the friendship, and realize that a great friendship in itself is a tremendous blessing.

We Can Always Turn Around

Some woman reading this book may feel as though she has already missed her opportunity for God's best. She acknowledges that she has let men take care of her financial needs in exchange for sexual favors. She recognizes that when she could have been talking this matter over with God and becoming the woman He created her to be, instead she was doing whatever she felt like doing and messed up plenty of relationships in the process. She knows that she has scared away some men who simply wanted to be her friend. So now she's asking, "Is it too late for me? Have I messed up too many times? Have I gotten too far away from God? Is my situation hopeless?"

The great thing about Christianity is that there is always room for another chance. It doesn't matter how badly or how often you may have messed up. It doesn't matter what you have done or with whom. It doesn't matter how many mistakes you've made, or even how badly you have sinned. We serve a God who will give us another chance. God doesn't give up on us.

I never use the GPS system on my phone. I'm sure my phone has that capability, but I've just never learned to use it. However, I use the navigation system in my car all the time. I use it whether I am driving in or out of town. No matter where I'm going, I enter the address in the system and let it guide me.

My wife, Sharon, asked one day, "What did we ever do before we had a GPS?"

"We got lost," I responded. "That's what we did."

As with most navigation systems, mine talks to me. It tells me to turn right in five hundred feet, or turn left now. I love that my GPS talks to me. Even if I momentarily forget where I'm going, the voice reminds me. Even if I get distracted, it keeps me focused. I may be distracted by the temptation to stop at a good restaurant I am approaching, but my GPS tells me to keep on going. My appetite is causing me to want to stop there, but my GPS reminds me I have a destination to reach and that restaurant isn't it.

Even if I go the wrong way, the navigational system keeps talking to me: "As soon as possible, make a U-turn. Turn left. Turn left. Turn left again." That's my GPS trying to get me back on track. Even though I was distracted by my desires, it doesn't give up on me. Instead, the voice reminds me, reroutes me, and redirects me in the way that I should go. Now, if my car can have a system that keeps talking to me and redirecting me until I'm on the right path, how much more will my heavenly Father keep talking to me, rerouting me, and giving me a chance to turn around and go in the right direction? Christ keeps redirecting us and will give us another chance.

MUTUALITY IS A MUST

At the same time, however, our faith has to be greater than just for the meeting. It also has to be a faith that can handle the mutuality of the relationship. Mutuality means that two different organisms come together and benefit each other without damaging either. When a man and woman come together, if one gets all of the benefits and the other gets damaged, that is not mutuality—that's a mess. It is not a relationship of faith.

Friendship-West Baptist Church Pastor Freddie Haynes has a sermon entitled, "Why Is My Loving You Killing Me?" If you are loving somebody and it is killing you, that is not mutuality. It is not of God, and it is not of faith. A relationship ought to be reciprocal, or mutual. It should involve give and take. If you are the one doing all of the giving, all of the loving, all of the serving, and all of the sacrificing, that is not of God. You need to have faith enough to know that this meeting was not of God and that there was no mutuality in it.

In our story from 1 Kings 17, we read about a meeting of two people whom God has brought together. The man brought blessings, and the woman brought bread. The man did not come to the table empty-handed. Similarly, God-directed women are not looking for undeveloped men who bring nothing to the relationship. This man, Elijah, brought blessing to the woman. He brought his personal relationship with God, an understanding of the Word of God, and the power of God into their relationship. When he showed up, this man became a role model for the woman's son. He attended to the boy's needs and, in fact, raised him up when he died. Elijah did all of this without getting or expecting any sexual favors from the boy's mother.

When Elijah came to Zarephath and found this woman whom he believed God had ordained for him to meet, he asked her for bread. He was not interested in a one-sided relationship, or a connection that was not mutual. In the midst of the drought (the dry situation), when Elijah first met the woman, he asked her for some water to drink. She was on her way to get the water when he called out, "And bring me a piece of bread too, please."

USE WHAT YOU'VE GOT

Remember, this woman has depleted resources. She is also in the midst of the drought, raising her son by herself. This request could have been the last straw for her. She could have gone off on Elijah, saying, "Wait one minute! You aren't from here, so evidently you don't know what we're going through. And you certainly don't know *me* and what *I'm* going through! How dare you ask me for bread!" No, she just responds to him with the simple truth: "I don't have any bread."

Now, this was perplexing for Elijah. He knew that God was behind this meeting. God had already told him that he was going to send this woman to him to feed him. And now that very woman was saying she had no bread; in fact, she had nothing with which to feed him. Now he was wondering, "How can I get from this woman what God said she would give me, when she hasn't got it?"

Now, I love the fact that this woman was not crying, complaining, or refusing to help this man because she had no bread. God is never going to command us to do something unless He gives us the ability to do it. If God gives us the *vision*, He always gives us the *pro*vision. But at this point in time, the woman had no bread. Yet instead of breaking down in tears or lashing out at the man in anger, she recounted to Elijah what she did have—sticks, a little flour, and a little oil. She also had knowledge in her head; she knew how to make her own bread.

This is a good lesson for all of us today. When we are facing a drought or an economic downturn in our own lives, it doesn't help to give up and sit down crying about what we don't have. It doesn't help us to become angry and lash out at others because we're feeling so miserable inside. As a single parent, even though it seems justified, it doesn't even help to carry around resentment against the baby's daddy or mommy because that person isn't there nor contributing financially. That resentment doesn't hurt the other person; it only hurts us, and keeps us from moving forward.

But it *would* help us greatly to think about what we *do* have. What are our assets? What can we bring to the situation? We need to look at what God has placed in our hands, what we have in our house, what we have in our head, and what we have in our heart. Then we need to take all of that, put it together, and make our own bread. Now, it might help to know that "bread" doesn't have to mean the bread we eat. When I was growing up, we used the word "bread" as a metaphor. When we said we were making bread, we didn't mean making bread to eat; we meant making money. We may be able to relate more to someone who needs to make money, as opposed to someone who needs to be able to bake some marble rye. The principles are the same.

PREACHER MANIPULATION?

So this woman pours her heart out to Elijah. She tells him that all she has is a little oil, a little flour, and a few sticks. She lets him know that her plan is to take the little she has and make one last small loaf of bread to share with her son—and then they will die. Now, we might be aghast at the response of this man of God. We might have expected him to respond by saying, "Here, let me give you what I have so that you can go buy what you need to keep going, at least a little longer." Or, "Wait, I'll take up a collection from among the good folk in this city. I'm sure they will want to help you."

But instead, Elijah, this man of God, tells her to go ahead and make the bread, but first to bring a small loaf of bread to him. Then, he said, she and her son could share what was left. On the surface, this sounds so selfish. What kind of man is this—that he would ask this single parent to make a meal for him first before taking care of her own needs or the needs of the child? This may even sound to us like a preacher who is trying to manipulate a vulnerable woman just to take something from her.

No, it was not that sort of a scenario at all. It wasn't a preacher trying to take something from this woman. It was a preacher who knew God's Word, and he was trying to set her up so that she would be in a position to receive something from God. Elijah knew that when we give to God first, God isn't going to let us beat Him in giving. If we take care of God's people, God takes care of our people. So she took care of this man of God, and later on, God took care of her.

CHOSEN FOR BLESSING

In biblical times, there was a man named Obadiah who sheltered fifty preachers in one place and fifty more in another place, and he showed up every day and fed them. He could afford to do that. God could have chosen a wealthy person like him to care for Elijah. But He didn't. There were thousands of prophets in the world and even a school of prophets. God could have chosen the prophets to care for Elijah. But He didn't. A short time earlier in Elijah's life, God sent ravens to bring him food to eat. God could have chosen the ravens to again provide for Elijah's needs. But He didn't. He chose a poor woman with few resources.

Why would God do something in such a hard way when there were other options available? Why would God ask something of her that she didn't have to give? Why would God expect so much from one who had so little? The answer is that God wanted to *bless* her and glorify His name.

Elijah knew the principle behind what God was asking, but God wanted the woman to give to Him first. It wasn't just *Elijah* asking her for bread. The prophet told her in 1 Kings 17:14, "For this is what the LORD, the God of Israel, says . . ." He wasn't just a man asking for a handout, but a prophet sharing the word from God with her. He knew that even though it sounded contrary to logic for her to give him something first, God would be true to His word. He knew that if the woman gave first to God, God would be sure that all of her needs were met.

We also face that same choice during those difficult times when our resources are depleted. Then we'll hear God saying, "Put Me first. I know your financial situation. I know how little you have. I know your needs. But put Me first." We must decide then to either consume the little that we have left and die, or contribute it and live.

We can ingest it and die, or we can invest it and live. When we give to God, we never give away. Giving to God is like making an investment, and when He pays us back, we'll find that it is always with interest. Again, God isn't going to let us beat Him in giving.

Rather than offering excuses about how little we have, if we give to God first, He will meet our needs. Sometimes God will bless us directly by pouring out the windows of heaven to shower us with blessings. Or we will be like a farmer who sows plenty of seed early on and then at harvest time reaps much. Or it may be like casting our bread on the water and then in a few days watching it come back to us. Philippians 4:19 (KJV) says, "But my God shall supply all your need according to his riches in glory by Christ Jesus." It doesn't say *some* of our needs, but *all* of them.

GOD MAKES IT LAST

But sometimes, God doesn't supply our needs by giving us something new. Instead, He provides by helping us preserve what we already have. Elijah told this widow in Zarephath that if she gave him something to eat first, God had promised, "The jar of flour will not be used up and the jug of oil will not run dry until the day the LORD sends rain on the land" (1 Kings 17:14). That was a great promise, but it required great faith on the part of the woman to receive that promise. Yet she rallied her faith and did what was asked of her. And just as God promised, "the jar of flour was not used up and the jug of oil did not run dry" (v. 16).

Note that God didn't give her more flour and oil. But the flour and oil she had did not run out. The jar of flour didn't overflow, but it never went empty. The jug of oil never overflowed, but it never went dry. God didn't give her provision; He gave her preservation. This woman was down to the very last that she had. She was going to use her last little bit of flour and oil to make a small loaf of bread for her and her son to eat before they died of starvation. Instead, upon hearing God's Word, she gave the last little bit she had to God, and God made her last *last*.

Some of us are blessed and don't even know it. We think blessings are always about getting new things, but sometimes blessings are just about maintaining what we already have. God may not give us a new car, but He keeps our old car running. He may not have given us a new job, but when everybody else was getting laid off, he kept us in our old job. He may not have given us a new outfit, but we're wearing an old outfit that came back into style and still looking good in it. He may not have given us new money, but we somehow still have a few dollars at the end of the month because He made our last *last*.

By looking at this story in 1 Kings, we understand that we must have faith that God is setting up a meeting for us with the right person at the right place and right time. We must have faith to wait for a relationship in which there is mutuality. And we must have faith for a miracle.

Some of us are out meeting with sugar daddies instead of waiting in faith for what God has planned. Sometimes we busy ourselves trying to get from others what God Himself wants to give us. By doing that, we miss out on the miracle.

GIVE GOD WHAT HE ASKS

This widow in Zarephath experienced a miracle. Verse 17 says, "Some time later the son of the woman who owned the house became ill. He grew worse and worse, and finally stopped breathing." This was a woman directed by God, a woman in a relationship that God had arranged, a woman who did exactly as God told her to do. Yet things still got worse and worse. Just because situations don't get better and better right away, that doesn't mean we are not in the plan of God. It doesn't mean that God is not watching over us or does not have a miracle waiting for us.

This woman didn't give up even after her son died, but she wasn't in denial either. She wasn't saying, "Oh, he's okay. I don't care what the doctor says; I know he's going to be alright." Denial does not bring deliverance. If we want deliverance, we have to deal with the situation—as it is, not as we wish it were. If our child is sick, then our child is sick. If our child is messing up in school, then our child is messing up in school. If our child is hanging with the wrong crowd, then our child is hanging with the wrong crowd. If our child is emotionally hurt, then our child is emotionally hurt. We cannot bring deliverance by denial. We have to deal with the situation in order to be delivered from it. We cannot fix what we do not face. This woman who had already lost her husband acknowledged that now she had also lost her only child.

She was grieving her loss deeply. She expressed her grief in anger to Elijah: "What do you have against me, man of God? Did you come to remind me of my sin and kill my son?" (1 Kings 17:18). Yet, even in the midst of all of the feelings of sorrow and anger that a grieving mother might naturally have, when Elijah said to her, "Give me your son," she didn't refuse to give him her child. She didn't cling to her son and say, "So what do you expect to do now? You can't help him now. You should have done something sooner while there was still hope. He's dead now. Don't you get it?! He's dead!" She didn't carry him off to the cemetery, place him in the ground, and walk away.

Instead, this broken woman let the man of God have the lifeless body of her son. She had already gotten to know Elijah. She already knew that he was a brother who brought something to their relationship. He was a brother who watched out for her and her son and made sure her needs were met. He was not a man who looked at this teary-eyed woman and said, "Well, I don't know what to tell you. This is all on you. You should have taken better care of the boy. This is your mess, not mine." No, he took her burden upon himself. He knew it was too much for her to bear, so he said, "Give him to me." Her faith prevailed over her feelings, and she let Elijah have her son.

Elijah took the boy to the upper room where he stayed. We have to be able to lift others up to another level. We can't always help them where they are. We have to be living above the mess they're in and be able to lift them up to a place where they can be helped.

We Don't Give Up on Our Children

Elijah did not see the dead child and then give up on him. He had faith that God could bring him back to life. More of us need the faith to persevere even when it seems that there is no hope. There are many young boys in the world who have become "sick"—sick on drugs, sick on alcohol, sick on crime, sick on hopelessness—and are living lifeless lives. We can't give up on them. We can't let them be buried alive. We need to go to them, take them in our arms, and let them know that our God is a God of restoration. Our God is a God of healing. Our God can make them live again.

Elijah did not try to help the boy from a distance. Even as Jesus stretched Himself out on the cross, Elijah stretched himself out on this boy. And he cried out to God on behalf of the child, "Lord my God, let this boy's life return to him!" (1 Kings 17:21). The first time he cried out, nothing happened. The second time, nothing happened. But the third time, life came back into the boy. Elijah didn't give up after the first time when nothing happened. He didn't give up the second time when nothing happened. He knew that we don't give up on our children. We pray for them until the miracle happens. His faith would not allow him to give up, no matter how long it took to see this boy restored. The ministry of restoration requires faith *and* perseverance.

To my single-parent friends, I say in a very personal way, "Don't give up on your children. Don't give up on your son. Don't give up on your daughter." Romans 8:11 lets us know that the same spirit that raised Christ from the dead dwells in us. That is a lot of power working in and through us. God can use us to bring others back to Life, back to Jesus.

Treat Children As the Blessings They Are

Some people do not feel free to minister to others because they are carrying a lot of guilt around with them. When the boy died, the widow said to Elijah, "Did you come to remind me of my sin and kill my son?" She thought bad things were happening because of her sin. Some mothers even go so far as to believe that their child is an ongoing consequence of their sins in the past. They think of their children as perpetual punishment for past perversions.

That is such a wrong, distorted view of children. Sin is having sex outside of wedlock. Whether it's fornication or adultery, *that* is the sin. Children are not the sin. Children are a natural consequence of the act of intercourse. It is a biological reality. But it is also a theological move of sovereignty.

When a man has sex with a woman, he releases millions of sperm within her. Yet from the millions of sperm, only one of them connects with the egg and produces a child. That child is one that God created. God brought that child into being. That child is exactly the person God wanted him or her to be—the right color, the right size, the right genes, and the right personality. That child is created by God with a destiny and purpose. Children never come as punishment, but as blessings. Psalm 127:3 says, "Children are a heritage from the Lord, offspring a reward from him." It doesn't say, "Children born in wedlock are a heritage from the Lord." No, God sees all children as blessings.

The problem is that the way we think of our children is the way we relate to them. If we think of our children as burdens, then we relate to them as burdens. If we think of them as punishment for sin, then we relate to them as punishment for sin. If we think of them as a consequence of wrong, then we look at them as a consequence of wrong. We don't embrace burdens. We don't love punishment. We don't praise consequences of wrong. So if we look at our children in those ways, we won't embrace, love or praise them.

But if we see children as God sees them—as blessings in our lives—then we treat them as blessings. We love them, treasure them, cherish them, care for them, hold them, provide for them, and even lay down our lives for them. We see them beautiful. We see them smart. We see them full of potential. And we look at them with eyes that reflect our positive feelings toward them. When they look into our eyes, they see love; when they hear our voices, they hear praise; when they experience our actions, they experience a sense of security that allows them to grow and thrive and become all that God intends for them to be.

LET THAT GUILT GO

It's interesting, though, when we look at our widow from Zarephath. This woman had not borne this child as a result of having sex out of wedlock. She had been married, but her husband had died. She wasn't looking upon her child as a consequence of sin. Yet when her son died, she still thought that she was being punished for her sins. She may not have committed fornication or adultery, but she had sinned in other ways. Romans 3:23 says that "all have sinned and fall short of the glory of God." So when something bad happened in this woman's life, she (like so many people) immediately thought it was because of her past sins.

We need to know that not all suffering is a consequence of sin. You can do everything right, and suffering will still come. Jesus *never* sinned, but He still suffered. This woman did something right, but she still suffered. She did everything within her means to care for her son after his father died, but she still suffered. She received the Word of God through the man of God, but she still suffered. She gave God first from the last little bit that she had, but she still suffered.

When we have come to God and asked Him to forgive us, when we have been washed clean by the blood of Jesus, and when we have made Jesus the Lord of our lives, we need to let go of that guilt. Micah 7:19 says that God will "hurl all our iniquities into the depths of the sea." Psalm 103:11-12 (KJV) says, "For as the heavens are high above the earth, so great is His mercy toward those who fear Him; as far as the east is from the west, so far has He removed our transgressions from us." If *God* chooses to cast our sins to a place that they can never again be found, why do *we* persist in keeping them in mind?

When memories of our sins and failures suddenly come to mind, we shouldn't dwell on them. Instead, we should immediately turn our hearts and minds to God and focus on Him as we cry out, "Thank You, Lord, for saving me! Thank You, God, that I am no longer the person I once was! Thank You for Your forgiveness! Thank You for Your salvation! Thank You for Jesus! Thank You for Your love! Thank You for Your grace!"

The devil loves it when Christians wallow in feelings of guilt and shame. We become of no use to God, and our faith plummets to the point that it isn't even as big as a mustard seed. If we are focusing on our sins of yesterday, we need to take back the peace that God has given us. We need to live in the NOW, not in the past. We need to live knowing that even though we have sinned, God loves us anyway and forgave us, and we are now washed fresh and clean by the blood that Jesus shed on Calvary.

ALL THINGS WORK FOR GOOD

The suffering the widow went through was not punishment. It was God setting her up for a greater miracle than she even imagined. Not only did she see her son brought back to life, but she also entered into a more personal relationship with God. As a result of her son growing ill and dying, she got to see God work a miracle through Elijah. It was only then that "the woman said to Elijah, "'Now I know that you are a man of God and that the word of the LORD from your mouth is the truth'" (1 Kings 17:24). She didn't know this during all of the time Elijah had stayed in her home and she served him. It was only after she went through a bad situation getting worse and worse and then seeing God's amazing restoration that she was able to make this declaration of faith: "Now I *know*." That's when she knew God's Word was true. That's when she embraced God in a new and personal way.

God was not letting her go through such a terrible ordeal to destroy her faith, but to take it to another level. What we are going through today isn't about our yesterdays, but about what God wants to do with us in our tomorrows. God wants us to know who He is and what His Word can do.

On Valentine's Day, 2014, the married couples from Eastern Star Church in Indianapolis went to a downtown hotel and celebrated the day together with other Christian couples. It was a great time. That day, however, a terrible snowstorm hit our city. In fact, I flew into Indianapolis and was headed home on the highway when the state transportation department closed it down. It took me two and a half hours to drive a route that would normally take me forty minutes. The snow and cold were terrible, but we showed up at the hotel for the party anyway.

Dr. David Hampton, pastor of Light of the World Christian Church in Indianapolis, happened to be staying at the same hotel. He wasn't there for our party, but he went there just to celebrate Valentine's Day with his wife. He called me from there and asked, "What's going on in this hotel? I keep seeing 'Eastern Star Church' all over the place. What's happening here?" I explained that the couples from our church were coming together to celebrate Valentine's Day with their spouses and other Christian couples.

He said, "Man, I'm in the same hotel. But let me tell you something. The valet people wrecked my car!" But he wasn't angry or upset. He was laughing and in good spirits.

I asked in disbelief, "You said they *wrecked* your car?"

"Yeah, they wrecked it."

"But you don't seem mad at all. If they wrecked my car, there would be a situation where some furniture would be moving. I know there's a storm and all that, but they should be careful."

"No, man, I'm not worried about that. They represent a five-star hotel. Since they wrecked my car because of the storm, not only is my room free, but they upgraded me to a suite. My dinner and all the other meals are free. All of my beverages are free. It's all fine."

My friend was getting great value out of a situation caused by a storm. Had there not been a storm, there would not have been a wreck. Had there not been a wreck, there would not have been an upgrade. Had the bad things not happened, he would not have experienced life as sweet as it was that night.

We need to know that the storms we are going through are signs that God is getting ready to upgrade us. Life is getting ready to be sweeter. There's a storm, but it's ushering in our miracle. There may be a wreck, but it will bring us good and not evil. When we see a storm coming, it isn't the time to abandon our faith, but to exercise it. Know then that the God who reigns on sunny days is the same God who reigns through the storms.

Our Father,

Great is Your faithfulness! Even when we can't see You, we know we can trust You. Even when we can't figure out what You are doing, we know we can have faith in You. Thank You, Lord, for saving us and freeing us from a guilty conscience through the blood of Jesus. Please remind us that You are working behind the scenes even when we can't see You. In Jesus' name, Amen.

CHAPTER 4

A FAITHFUL SINGLE PARENT: DESTINY'S CHILD

In the sixth month of Elizabeth's pregnancy, God sent the angel Gabriel to Nazareth, a village in Galilee, to a virgin named Mary. She was engaged to be married to a man named Joseph, a descendant of King David. Gabriel appeared to her and said, "Greetings, favored woman! The Lord is with you!"

Confused and disturbed, Mary tried to think what the angel could mean. "Don't be afraid, Mary," the angel told her, "for you have found favor with God! You will conceive and give birth to a son, and you will name him Jesus."

(Luke 1:26-31 NLT)

GOD CHOSE THE VIRGIN MARY

God has had only one Son: "God so loved the world that he gave his one and only Son, that whoever believes in him shall not perish but have eternal life" (John 3:16). In God's wisdom and providential design, this one Son was conceived in the womb of a single woman. This God is omnipotent, omniscient, and omnipresent. He is all-powerful, all-knowing, and ever-present. He could have chosen any way to bring His Son into the world. And He could have used any person at all (or no person at all) to be involved in this magnificent event. But God chose to use a single woman.

As I've stated previously, I believe that life starts at conception, not at birth. When Jesus, God's Son, was conceived, his mother Mary was not married yet. When Jesus entered into Mary's womb, He made her into a single parent. This was a young virgin woman. Then suddenly, she was pregnant. I've wondered why God chose to bring Jesus into the world this way. This was not a normal event. I would not have expected God to do it this way. This was unprecedented.

There have been other times that God has miraculously intervened in a woman's life and caused her to get pregnant. But in all of those instances, the woman was married. God intervened in Sarah's life in her old age, and she got pregnant; but she was married. God intervened in Hannah's life after her years of barrenness, and she conceived; but she was married. God intervened in Elizabeth's life after she and her husband had given up on the idea of having children, and she got pregnant; but she was married.

But when it came to God's only Son, He decided to use a single woman. This was not a whim of God's—something He simply decided to do one day and Mary happened to come to mind. The Old Testament prophet Isaiah prophesied that a *virgin* would conceive and give birth to God's Son (Isaiah 7:14). This virgin birth was in God's plan from the beginning of time. God *chose* Mary to become a single parent to bear His Son Jesus.

THE LIFE OF MARY

Even though the Bible doesn't give us a lot of specific details about Mary's life, historical records of the life and culture of Jewish women in that time period allow us to piece together what is likely a fairly accurate account of this young woman. Scholars believe that Mary was between the ages of twelve and fourteen because that was the common age range in which young women were married in those days. In all likelihood, she grew up in Nazareth, an insignificant village often held in disdain by others. In John 1:46, before meeting Jesus personally, Nathaniel heard that He was from Nazareth and scoffed, "Nazareth! Can anything good come from there?"

Scholars also believe that Mary was poor—a peasant. Without the conveniences we take for granted today, women worked tirelessly to draw water, grind wheat or other grains to make flour, bake bread, press olives to get oil for cooking and for the small lamps they used at night, care for their families, make material and sew all of their clothes, work in the gardens or farms, and do the endless chores that were simply a part of daily life then. The Romans also occupied Palestine, and the Jews were an oppressed people, which only added to their burdens.

God sent an angel to announce His plan to Mary. The angel He sent passed by the queen of Ethiopia, Pharaoh's wife, Mrs. Caesar Augustus, Mrs. Pilate, Mrs. Herod, and all of the other important women of that day. Instead, the angel went straight to this poor, young single girl living under oppression in an unimportant place. I believe God made that choice then because He knew that in twenty-first century America, 60 percent of the children being born would be born to single parents. God knew that in twenty-first century America, 80 percent of the Black children being born would be born to single parents. God knew that in twenty-first century America, 70 percent of households would be headed by single parents.

God wanted to provide an example for all of these single parents so that they could see how Mary handled this situation and gain reassurance that they would be able to handle it too. He wanted to offer a model of single motherhood so that when single mothers today feel like giving up, they can look back at the single woman He chose to carry His own child.

MARY SAID YES

Think about how Mary must have felt in the midst of this situation. Getting a message from an angel was not in her plans for her life. She was already engaged to the carpenter Joseph. In those days, Joseph may have approached Mary's father to initiate this relationship, or the parents may have arranged the marriage; but a contract had been signed, and Mary was now considered Joseph's bride. She belonged to him and no other. If she had sexual intercourse with anyone else from then on, she would be considered an adulterer.

They were now waiting during a period of engagement that could last up to a year. During this time, she was undoubtedly dreaming about what her wedding day would be like—when she would leave her parents' home, go to be united with Joseph, and start their new life together. Undoubtedly, she was deciding who would be her bridesmaids, thinking about the dress she would wear, planning how she would wear her hair, and choosing the makeup or jewelry she might wear to look special. She already had a plan for her life. Her plan included settling into Joseph's house, having his babies, and living a happily married life. But all of her great plans changed when she got pregnant.

It is hard for us today to imagine the stigma and repercussions for a single woman at that time who got pregnant. Women were not formally educated, and there were no jobs available for single women to support themselves and their children. In most cases, if a quick marriage could not be arranged, the woman was simply sent away to somehow fend for herself. With the family shunning her and the community rejecting her, her desperation to meet basic needs for herself and her child could lead her to become a prostitute or even to sell herself into slavery. And then there was always the possibility that she could be stoned to death for her sin of adultery.

When Mary said yes to God's plan, she had no way of knowing what would happen to her or to her baby. When she said yes to God, she was literally placing herself in God's hands, not knowing what her future would hold. Mary was exhibiting great courage and faith in God. She didn't go into deep depression, slit her wrist, or jump off a building because her plans changed. She knew that an unchanging God would help her deal with her changing plans.

PLANS CHANGE

We all encounter changes to our plans during our lifetimes. It is how we deal with those changes that determines the course of our future. Most of the people we know who are successful in their areas of expertise were not initially planning to get into those particular career fields. Most successful people planned to go into one area, but their plans got changed. Yet they found success in their new direction.

Denzel Washington planned to be an NFL football player until he became a successful actor instead. Will Smith planned to be the greatest rapper of all time until he found out that he could get $20 million for every movie he was in. Plans change.

It is interesting to ask people in various fields what their majors were in college. Very often, you will hear that they majored in one area, but now they are doing something entirely different. One might say, "My major was political science," but today he is running a chain of restaurants. Another may say, "I majored in music," but she is currently directing a homeless shelter. Truthfully, when I was in college, I majored in sin and ungodliness, hanging with the wrong people and being in the wrong place at the wrong time doing the wrong thing. But thankfully, God changed my plans!

We often see single parents fantasizing about married life. They look at married couples around them and say, "They're so happy. That's what I wanted." But the fact is that most married people are not with the person who was part of their original plan. My wife and I have been married for twenty-seven years, but I was not her first choice. Now, in my humble opinion, I believe that I was her *best* choice, but I wasn't her *first* choice. Plans change. But our unchanging God will help us with changing plans. Just because it didn't work out with the baby's daddy or the baby's mama, it doesn't mean that marriage will never happen because of losing that one person. Plans change.

Mary's plans were changed for her, and now she became a model for single motherhood. Think about how hard that would have been for her to have to tell her fiancé and family about her condition. She was a woman without any money or options. Mary was from a religious family, so she knew they would be both angry and ashamed of her. The man to whom she was engaged was a righteous man. She knew that this change in her would be devastating to him. She also understood full well the consequences of her unwed pregnancy under Jewish law.

SEEK GODLY SUPPORT

Some young women in our own society can relate to some degree to what Mary must have been feeling. A single woman who has had to tell her mother that she's pregnant understands those feelings. To see this woman whom she loves begin to cry, and know that she has broken her mother's heart, hurts her deeply. When she tells her father, he becomes irate—first wanting to kill the boy involved and then threatening to disown his daughter. When she tells her youth leader at church, she hopes to find compassion, but instead she is asked to leave the youth group and withdraw from the junior usher board. Then the pastor makes her stand up before the congregation and confess her sin. It wasn't demanded of her and the boy who impregnated her, but just her—alone. She feels exposed, worthless, disgraced, and unloved. She understands how Mary must have felt.

Mary, however, set a good example for other young women in her condition. She went looking for the kind of support that she needed to help her at this critical time. She knew that she needed to surround herself with people who would rejoice with her over her baby, people who could give her good advice, and people who would love her unconditionally.

Sadly, some young women today get their advice and information from television instead of trusted advisers. They don't understand that most television shows are for entertainment, not enlightenment. So they watch the incredibly messed-up people in dysfunctional relationships on reality TV and think that life must inevitably be like that. They watch programs about NBA wives who aren't always even married to NBA players and NFL wives who aren't married to NFL players, and they think this is what relationships are like. They watch dramatic wealthy wives from big cities and learn from them what they *think* it means to be married. They listen to TV psychologists talking to miserable people in miserable situations and try to get advice from what they hear. In fact, some young women spend so much time in front of the TV that they lose sight of reality. They can no longer tell the difference between what's real and what's phony.

Thankfully, Mary took a different approach. She didn't look to the world to learn about herself, about God, about motherhood, about marriage, or about life. First of all, she was able to keep in mind all that the angel had told her when he came to announce that she would carry God's Son within her. The angel was simply a messenger who brought a word to her from God. God knew that people would be skeptical of Mary, would not believe her, would shun her, and call her a slut or whore. So, even before all of that happened, God sent an angel to tell Mary what *He* thought about her.

WHAT DOES *GOD* SAY?

When the angel appeared, his first words to Mary were, "Greetings, you who are highly favored! The Lord is with you" (Luke 1:28). Immediately she knew that the angel was not coming to condemn her, but to praise her. He let her know that she had found favor with God and God was with her. Just in case she missed that part of the message the first time, the angel told her not to be afraid and repeated, "You have found favor with God" (Luke 1:30). Then he told her that among all of the women on earth, in all of the time periods of history, she was the person God chose to bring His own Son into the world. This was terrifying and awesome news wrapped into one message. But the angel made Mary feel comfortable enough to ask him a question, and he answered it so that she would know more of what to expect.

It's important for all of us today to learn more about what God thinks of us. Psalm 139:14 tells us that we are "fearfully and wonderfully made." Verse 13 lets us know that God Himself created us and knit us together in our mothers' wombs. Verse 10 tells us that no matter where we go in this life, God's right hand is there to hold us fast. God loves each one of us more than we can ever begin to imagine. He knows our weaknesses, faults, and failures, yet He still loves us. Psalm 139:16 says, "Your eyes saw my unformed body; all the days ordained for me were written in your book before one of them came to be." When God creates each one of us, He does so with a plan and purpose for our lives.

It is so important that we know how God feels about us so we can better embrace His plan and purpose for our lives. When we reject what God thinks and accept what others think as truth, we focus on the superficial rather than on what is truly important. We compare ourselves with physical images that the world keeps before us—images of beautiful women and handsome men—and we become miserable because we don't look like that. We listen to the criticism of others and believe that if they said it about us, it must be true. So we devalue ourselves and become vulnerable to those who will say anything to us just to get what they want from us. We leave ourselves open to dysfunctional relationships. Until we accept who we are in God, who we are from God's perspective, we cannot bring our true selves into a relationship nor live life to the fullest.

That's why some Christian women are missing out on God's best for them. These women know the Lord, are involved in church, and spend time in prayer. They also have an education, good jobs, and meaningful lives. And, of course, they still have a natural desire for marriage and children. Yet when a good, honest Christian man approaches them, they won't give him the time of day. The underlying reason is that, in spite of how they've got it together in every area of their lives, they feel unworthy of a man of that caliber. They may not even know that consciously, but their subconscious minds are controlling them, and they behave based on those deep negative thoughts about themselves. So when a lowlife man comes along, they open themselves up to him because, deep inside, they think that is all they deserve. They don't see themselves as God sees them, so they are not open to the blessings that God has for them.

That is why it is so crucial to have a good support system. We need somebody with the knowledge of God's Word who can remind us who we are from God's perspective. If we don't know and receive what God thinks about us, we will believe what the person next to us thinks about us or what our friends or family think about us, and their perceptions may not be at all true. That's why we need a messenger from God to let us know what He thinks about us and remind us that He has a plan for us. This person must be able to tell us that the reason we are going through a certain situation is not because God doesn't love us, but because He has a plan for us. Mary's plan failed. What she thought was going to come to pass didn't happen. But God's plan never fails.

WHEN PLAN "A" FAILS

It's important to remember that Mary didn't get depressed or give up because her plan failed. She didn't tell God's messenger, "But I don't WANT to carry God's Son. I don't WANT to go through all the difficulties that will come. I don't WANT to do this. I just want to marry Joseph, as I planned, to have *his* children, and to be a good wife and mother. *Please* ask God to choose someone else." Instead, Mary accepted the fact that her plan was not going to materialize and embraced God's plan for her life.

Dr. Theron Williams, pastor of Mount Carmel Church in Indianapolis, has a sermon entitled "Making It on Plan B." He points out that most people give up when Plan A fails because they don't have a Plan B. Things didn't go the way they thought, so they get depressed and think, "What's the use? Nothing ever works out for me anyway."

Dr. Williams says that we have to be willing to accept Plan B because oftentimes, *our* Plan B is *God's* Plan A. Plan B is what God had in mind for us all the time. If we can just let go of Plan A, embrace Plan B, and move on with enthusiasm, we will be able to see that God had our best interests at heart all along. We lost what we didn't really need and gained what we always really wanted.

When the messenger came to Mary, he not only talked about how God felt towards her, but he also talked about her baby. He told her so many wonderful things about this child: "He will be great and will be called the Son of the Most High. The Lord God will give him the throne of his father David, and he will reign over Jacob's descendants forever; his kingdom will never end" (Luke 1:32-33). Now, Mary couldn't see any of this; she had to believe God. That's where her faith had to come in.

Just because we can't see something, that doesn't mean it isn't going to happen. When God says something is going to happen, it doesn't matter that we cannot see it at the time. If God says it will happen, it will happen. In the meantime, that's our opportunity to demonstrate our faith in Him, our hope based on His Word, and our expectation that He is a good God who gives good gifts to His children. We stand on God's promise in Jeremiah 29:11, "'For I know the plans I have for you," declares the Lord, "plans to prosper you and not to harm you, plans to give you hope and a future.'"

Even if we can't *see* all the good things that God has spoken about our children, we have to believe what God has said about them. In Psalm 127:3, God says, "Children are a heritage from the LORD, offspring a reward from him." Children are a blessing. They are a reward from God. Proverbs 22:6 says, "Train up a child in the way he should go: and when he is old, he will not depart from it." We shouldn't go around saying, "Well, I don't see it. I trained him up right, and he's just doing his own thing." It isn't about what we see, but what we believe, that really counts. Do we have enough faith that God will keep His promises about our children?

NEVER SAW IT COMING

I am a product of a single parent. When I was very young, my father left us and never looked back. My mother raised us by herself and trained us up in the way we should go. There were four of us children, and my mother worked two jobs to make ends meet. As a youngster, I went through what a lot of young people experience when there is a breakdown in the family. I had emotional, behavioral, and anger issues, along with so many negative things happening within me.

But I changed when I gave my life to Jesus and was filled with the Holy Spirit. God called me to preach, and I am now pastoring one of the greatest churches in the world. I travel around the country and to various places in the world, where I preach the gospel. And I am one of the most amazed men in America; I'm amazed that people want to hear me preach. People fly me in from all over the place because they want to know what I think about what God's Word says. That amazes me.

Every now and then, when people see what God is doing in my life, they ask my mother, "Did you see this coming?" Her response is always, "I never saw it coming." Then she and my grandmother begin talking about all of the faults they saw in me and bring up all of the things I did wrong as a child—things that kept them from ever envisioning my life as it is now. Sometimes, when they get carried away, I stop them and point out that the person wasn't asking for details about my yesterdays.

Every now and then, I catch my mother just staring at me, and then she says, "Jeff, (she's the only person with permission to call me "Jeff"), I never saw it coming." Even if we don't see it coming, that doesn't mean that it isn't coming. It doesn't matter what your child looks like, what he or she is going through, or what issues you are facing: if God says good things will happen, they are going to happen.

God Holds Us Tighter in the Storms

I know it's hard. I am not trying to belittle anyone's situation. When our plans have failed, when the person we thought we would be with walks out on us, when family and friends turn away from us, when we're facing all of life's challenges alone, I know it's hard. We have to believe just as Mary did that God isn't going to forsake us . God isn't going to fail us. We must have that confidence, that faith, to get us through the times when we can't see clearly to the time when it all opens up before us.

There was a night in December of 2013 that I will always remember. It was a cold, snowy night, and I was driving my son, K. J., to a youth meeting at church. We were approaching an intersection in which a highway and two major streets meet. Traffic there was flowing east and west, north and south, and southwest and northeast, and it all converged in that one spot. Not only was it snowing, but there was also ice and sleet, so the roads had become treacherous. As we approached this intersection, I saw the light turn yellow and put on my brakes. But as the light turned red, my car was still going forward. It was heading towards this convergence of cars, and there was nothing I could do about it. I did what I was supposed to do, but my car was out of control. My son was sleeping next to me.

As my car kept moving, my seatbelt suddenly began to tighten on me. I didn't even know my car had the capability of doing that, but it happened automatically. I didn't push a button, press down on any lever, or turn anything. All I did was put on the brakes. We were headed towards a crash, and my seatbelt began tightening. It tightened so much on K. J., in fact, that it woke him up. He had been sleeping through the storm, but now he was awake, held securely by his seatbelt. My car was telling me, "When you're headed towards trouble ahead, I'm not going to let you go. I'm going to hold you even tighter." Now, if a car will do that, certainly our God will do that! When storms are happening in our lives and everything is out of our control, God doesn't let us go. He just holds us tighter!

LOOKING FOR GOOD, NOT PERFECT

In Mary's support system, she also had a man who was right with God. Now, some single women are so angry with the previous man in their lives, they don't want to even think about men. They've had it with men. You may be among those saying right now, "I don't need a man." But if you stop to think about it, what you are really saying is, "I don't need that last man who was in my life." That last man may have been a dog in disguise. He ignored you, mistreated you, and walked out on you. You're right, you don't need that. But that is not what a real man does. I know it's hard to get over a wounded heart, but it's important not to harden our hearts and put up a "No Trespassing" sign. We must stay open to what God might have for us. We have to remember that we were operating on Plan A, but God's best for us is Plan B. We have to keep our lives open to a new plan.

If you are a single woman, God may have a *real* man in store for you. He may have a man who will love you and support you. This man will embrace the opportunity to be a father, not run from it. This man will be a role model for your son and show your daughter what a real man looks like. This man will bring something to you and your children, not simply try to take from you all that he can.

Mary had a man like this. Joseph was a good man who cared about her feelings and lived to please God. One translation said he was righteous. That doesn't mean he was perfect, but that he was right with God. When we come to God through His Son Jesus Christ, we don't become perfect, but we become right with God.

It is really critical that we choose our life partner based on his or her relationship with God. The person must be right with God, because if not, he or she will not be right with us either. If the person is wrong with God, the person is wrong for us as well.

If we are looking for Mr. Perfect, or Ms. Perfect, however, we will never find anyone like that for our support system because that perfection does not exist. Some women ignore their Mr. Right because they are looking for Mr. Perfect. Some men miss their Ms. Right because they are looking for Ms. Perfect.

RIGHTEOUS DOESN'T MEAN ALWAYS BEING RIGHT

One of the things that distinguished Joseph as a righteous man was his acknowledgement of personal wrong. If a man believes he is always right, something isn't right. Any woman who thinks she is never wrong is definitely wrong. But Joseph was a righteous man, so he could change his mind about something when he realized he was wrong.

This is the way it happened for him: We know that he and Mary were engaged and looking forward to their wedding. Everything was going fine until Mary turned up pregnant. When that happened, Joseph decided that he had to break it off with her. He didn't want to shame her or make her a target of ridicule in the community, so he wasn't going to drag her out in front of everyone to accuse her of adultery. He was just going to quietly send her away.

We have to understand where Joseph was coming from so that we don't judge him for his initial response. First of all, Joseph felt that Mary had broken their covenant. They were betrothed to each other, and everyone saw them in a committed relationship. But Mary got pregnant, and Joseph knew the baby wasn't his because they had never had sex. The only logical explanation was that Mary had been with someone else. How could he enter into marriage with a woman who was already cheating on him?

Second, Joseph was a man who kept the laws of God. In his mind, Mary had broken God's law by sleeping with another man. If he stayed with her and swept her sin under the carpet, so to speak, he would be almost as guilty as she was in the eyes of the law. How could he betray God by being faithful to this woman?

And third, if Joseph had decided that he was going to marry the woman regardless, then he was sullying his own reputation. The people in the community saw him as a righteous man, a man who loved God and kept His laws. If they pushed up the wedding date and everyone noticed that Mary was pregnant, they would naturally assume that Joseph had broken God's law and slept with this woman out of wedlock. How could Joseph allow his good name to be tarnished when he had done nothing wrong? Joseph was in a difficult situation. There was no perfect answer for him, but he was trying to do the right thing and maintain a right spirit.

Not only had Mary's plans changed, but when he heard of her pregnancy, Joseph's plans changed, too. That type of change would have happened even if Mary had gotten pregnant by Joseph. The dynamics of the relationship would still have changed, and their plans would never have been exactly as they were before. Before Mary got pregnant, Joseph was proud of his virgin bride and could hardly wait to be with her. It was critical in those days that the bride be a virgin. In fact, in many places, after the new husband and wife slept together on their wedding night, it was the custom of the times to make public the bloody cloth sheet the woman lay upon that would verify she had been a virgin. Since Mary was pregnant, that changed everything.

FIND A MATE WHO LISTENS TO GOD

In the midst of all of Joseph's turmoil, after he made the decision to quietly divorce Mary and send her away to fulfill the law but not bring her greater shame, an angel appeared to him as he slept. In the dream, the angel said to Joseph, "Joseph son of David, do not be afraid to take Mary home as your wife, because what is conceived in her is from the Holy Spirit. She will give birth to a son, and you are to give him the name Jesus, because he will save his people from their sins" (Matthew 1:20-21). When he woke up, Joseph was willing to obey God, whatever the consequences. He went to Mary and told her that he had been wrong. He apologized for misjudging her, and he took her to himself as his wife.

But his plans had been changed. It wasn't just that they had to move up the wedding date. Joseph knew now that people in the community were undoubtedly talking about him, pointing a finger at him and accusing him of having sex with Mary before their wedding. To make it even worse, Joseph was not even allowed to consummate their marriage. He was not able to sleep with his wife until Jesus was born. That is *not* the way Joseph had planned it.

Notice in this story, however, that it was not Joseph's woman who was able to show him that he was wrong. She undoubtedly had tried, but who's going to believe a woman who shows up pregnant and then gives some wild story about an angel appearing and her baby being God's baby? No, it wasn't Mary who was able to get Joseph to change his mind. Joseph didn't believe this story until God helped him to see that it was true. There are some times when only God can change a person's mind.

There are some women who have been berating their baby's daddy for ten years. Every chance she gets, the woman reminds him of how badly he treated her, tells him that he's no good, and demands more support from him. But in ten years, he has still not changed. Sometimes, only God can change a person. There are times when we need to talk to a partner about God, but there are still other times when we need to talk to God about a partner. Even when a partner won't listen to us, there are times when God can get through to him or her.

IT'S A PACKAGE DEAL

Another indication that Joseph was a righteous man was his acceptance of not only Mary, but her baby too. Tragically, there are some women who are willing to say to a man, "Well, if you won't take us both, at least take me." She is willing to sacrifice her baby just to get a man. She is willing to let someone else raise the child she carried in her womb just to get a man who is unwilling to take in her baby as well.

Sure, it will be more of a challenge if children are involved, but how can he truly love the woman and not be willing to also love her child? If his heart doesn't have the capacity to embrace them both, it is too small to love any woman the way she needs to be loved. It doesn't matter how much money he makes or how many promises he makes, a mother should never be willing to give up her baby for the sake of a man. If that happens, neither of them is worthy to receive that child as a blessing from God, a reward from the Lord.

The single mother must always let an interested man know that she comes only as a package deal. In fact, if children have the right place in a mother's heart, she won't wait until the fifth date or tenth date to bring them up in conversation. Her love for them and excitement over them can't be held back. She should never behave as though she is ashamed of them; instead, she should always speak about them lovingly and with pride.

She doesn't have to spend an entire evening talking about her children as though she has nothing else in her brain, but very early on in the relationship, she has to say, "And I have two adorable children"—or three or four, or whatever the number is. If that makes the man end the date early and never call again, then he wasn't the right one for her anyway.

A BABY DOESN'T MAKE A MARRIAGE

Did you ever stop to think about the fact that the right man in Mary's life was not the child's father? The man who raised Jesus was not His biological father. Now, I'm old-school about many things, but I don't believe that a woman should marry a man just because he got her pregnant. This is strictly my opinion, but I think that marriage is hard enough even if a woman marries the right man at the right time. To marry someone *just* because a baby resulted from having sex with him is a poor foundation for a marriage that will last.

Genesis 2:23-24 says, "The man said, 'This is now bone of my bones and flesh of my flesh; she shall be called "woman," for she was taken out of man.' That is why a man leaves his father and mother and is united to his wife, and they become one flesh." Why does a man leave his parents and unite with a wife? There is no mention in these verses that it's because there is a baby on the way.

The reason for a man to marry a particular woman is because she has become such a part of him that he cannot imagine life without her. He loves her even as he loves himself. She is bone of his bone and flesh of his flesh. They are united in spirit and in soul; therefore, he chooses for them to be united as one flesh as well and be together for the rest of their lives. A woman should not want a marriage based only on the fact that they had sex one night and a baby was made. She should want to be loved deeply and intimately and to know that she has a place in her man's heart that is only for her.

BEING ON THE SAME PAGE

I'm real when I talk with my sons. They range in age from seventeen to the oldest who just turned twenty-six. Just because I'm a pastor, that doesn't mean that we are always walking on holy ground. We don't spend our Sundays in church and our weekdays in heaven. I know the world in which my family and I live. I know that our Plan A doesn't always work out. I know that, even among Christians, what we plan, what we want, what we strive for, what we've always dreamed, doesn't always work out. We live in a fallen world and life isn't always perfect. But I've told my sons, "As best you can, be sure that when you have children, they are always living with you in your home."

When children live in our home, we determine what church they go to, what image of God they are presented with, what TV shows they watch, what music they listen to, what extracurricular activities they are involved in, what people they are exposed to in the home, what atmosphere they grow up in, what environment they live in day by day, and what messages they are getting about family, God, life, and the world. I pointed out to my sons that it would be very frustrating for them to send money to support their children in another residence, where they have no voice in all of those matters that are crucial for a child's development.

In Mary's situation, the man God brought into her life was not the child's father, but—after being certain this marriage was God's will for him—he was willing not only to receive Mary into his life, but to receive her child as well. When this child was born, Joseph joined the child's mother in naming him. When the angel appeared to Mary, he told her that the child was to be called "Jesus." Matthew 1:25 says that Joseph "gave him the name Jesus."

The reason they were on the same page regarding the name is because they were both listening to the voice of God as He spoke to them through an angel. They were both listening to the same God. If one parent is listening to the Lord God Almighty but the other parent is listening to another god, there will always be strife when it comes to the children. One will want to call the child one name, while the other has a different name already picked out. One will see within the child what God sees within him or her, while the other sees something completely different from the perspective of another god. One will long for the day that this child knows the Lord personally, while the other will try to lead him or her to another god. Strife is inevitable if the parents are divided about the identity of God.

STEP ASIDE AND WATCH GOD WORK

In this story about how Jesus came into the world, we note that Mary always maintained her integrity and dignity. After Mary became pregnant, even though she knew that Joseph did not believe her story and planned to leave her, never once did she try to change his mind. She wasn't showing up on the construction site where he was working, desperately saying, "We've got to talk about this thing. You said you would marry me. I've told you how this happened. Don't you believe me? Are you just going to cast me aside like some dog? Maybe you aren't the man I thought you were anyhow." She wasn't sitting outside his home, watching to see if there were any other women coming now to see Joseph. She wasn't slashing his chariot wheels to get back at him. She wasn't putting him down to anyone who would listen to her. She went on with her life, finding support elsewhere when she did not get it from him.

The great thing about Mary's response is that when she stepped aside, God was able to step in. If Mary had been crying and nagging Joseph all the time, he would have tuned out and not have been able to even hear the voice of God. But when Mary was silent, God was able to speak and work in Joseph's heart. Mary kept her composure and gave Joseph space to hear God. There were undoubtedly times in their relationship when Mary was upset and Joseph gave her space to hear God.

It is so important for married couples to learn how to support each other in this way. The eloquent preacher Gardner C. Taylor has said that the difference between a good marriage and a bad marriage is knowing when to leave the room.

My wife and I have been married for twenty-seven years, and we have four children. We don't have a perfect marriage, but we have a healthy marriage. Some people think that being a pastor somehow negates him from being a man. They think, "Well, of course you have a good marriage. You spend all your time praying and reading the Bible. You're a man of God." Yes, I do pray. Yes, I do read the Bible. Yes, I am a man of God. But I am still a man. As Paul and Barnabas told the people in Acts 14:15, "We too are only human, like you." The apostle James wrote in James 5:17, "Elijah was a human being, even as we are." Being people who serve God does not change the fact that we are still human beings. Even Jesus Himself faced temptations because although He was fully divine, He was also fully human. Hebrews 4:15 (KJV) says, "For we have not an high priest which cannot be touched with the feeling of our infirmities; but was in all points tempted like as we are, yet without sin."

As a man, I face the same temptations that all men face. But when it comes to making our marriage work, I have learned to leave the room. I know that if my wife is going off about something and I don't agree with her, our discussion will escalate to an argument and our argument will quickly escalate to a fight. And then it isn't the preacher or man of God who is showing up in the room; it's just Jeffrey Johnson, a man like any other man. And I do know how to play that role all too well. I'm not the only one who keeps our arguments in check either. My wife also knows how to keep us from crossing that line from attacking an issue to attacking each other. We've learned over the years how to keep our marriage healthy.

A TRUE MENTOR

Another part of Mary's support system was her cousin Elizabeth. When the angel appeared to Mary, after all of the amazing news he told her about herself and her baby, he also added, "Even Elizabeth your relative is going to have a child in her old age, and she who was said to be unable to conceive is in her sixth month" (Luke 1:36). Remember that Mary didn't have a lot of support. She wasn't skipping around the village, announcing, "I'm going to have God's baby." First of all, she was far too humble to behave in that way. Second, as an engaged woman, she could have been condemned for adultery and stoned. Third, she knew that no one would believe that. Who would? Short of an angel appearing with a message from God, there is no reason in the world that any sane person would believe that story. They would have thought that Mary was either lying or had become mentally imbalanced. Hers was not a story that she or her family would have been excited to announce.

Yet Mary still needed support. So she went to someone who was also pregnant, but was further along than she was. This is a useful lesson for some of us who keep waiting for someone to show up for us when we're hurting. We sit at home crying, "Nobody cares about me. They should know what I'm going through. They should be here for me." But Mary didn't sit at home wallowing in self-pity. She didn't have anyone coming to her, but she went out to find the help she needed.

There is a little bit of symbolism in this portion of the story too. "Judea" is an adaptation of the word "Judah," which means "praise." And Judea was in the hill country. Mary didn't choose to go *down* into discouragement and depression. She chose instead to go *up* to a place of praise.

She went there to find an older woman who had something special that was placed in her by God. This woman was also further along with what God was doing in her life than Mary. The people Mary left behind couldn't identify with her. They didn't understand what was in her because they didn't have anything in themselves. Mary needed someone who had experienced God in a personal way just as she had, and one who was further along in her walk with God. She knew that woman would have something meaningful to share with her.

Mary was not disappointed. When she showed up at Elizabeth's house, this older woman didn't begin harassing her. She didn't yell, "What are you doing pregnant? You know that you and Joseph should have waited. This is a shame to our family and a disgrace to our God. And what are you doing coming here? Don't think you're going to do something like this and then get any sympathy from me." No, Elizabeth didn't condemn her; she comforted her. She didn't judge her; she rejoiced with her. She didn't talk down to her; she used her voice to lift her up. She recognized that God was doing something with Mary. Luke 1:41-45 says,

> When Elizabeth heard Mary's greeting, the baby leaped in her womb, and Elizabeth was filled with the Holy Spirit. In a loud voice, she exclaimed: "Blessed are you among women, and blessed is the child you will bear! But why am I so favored, that the mother of my Lord should come to me? As soon as the sound of your greeting reached my ears, the baby in my womb leaped for joy. Blessed is she who has believed that the Lord would fulfill his promises to her!"

TESTS OF A TRUE MENTOR

Elizabeth was older and more mature spiritually than Mary, but she could humble herself and lift Mary up, telling her (v. 42), "Blessed are you among women!" And then this young girl who had accepted God's plan for her life in spite of all of the criticism she might face and the hardships she might endure heard this mature, godly woman whom she respected say to her, "Why am I so favored that the mother of my Lord should come to me?" Perhaps feeling ashamed due to the stigma of being a single mother and afraid of how others would respond to her, Mary had only hoped against hope that she might find some little bit of support from Elizabeth. But now she heard this woman honoring *her*, respecting *her*, and feeling that *her* presence was a blessing. We can only imagine the joy this brought to Mary's heart. Now someone understood and believed in her. Someone saw what was happening to her as a good thing. Someone helped her to be able to move from a place of shame to one of joy.

Elizabeth was saying to Mary the same thing that the angel had said to her. And the same is true for us. When a messenger is saying one thing and our mentor is saying something else, that is confusing. But when both the messenger and our mentor are hearing from God and saying the same thing, that's when we know we have confirmation and direction for our lives.

Mary could even literally *see* the work of God in Elizabeth's life. Mary had only just become pregnant with Jesus. She had only just gotten Jesus in her, so she wasn't showing yet. Most people didn't know yet that Jesus was in her. Likewise, when we first accept Christ as our personal Savior and He comes to reside in us, it doesn't always show a lot at the beginning. But over time, Jesus' presence makes a difference in us.

God had been doing something special in Elizabeth's life for six months. She was now providing tangible evidence that something new and wonderful was going on inside of her. She didn't even have to *say* anything because people could actually *see* that something was happening in her.

If we have a mentor, we should be able to *see* something in that person. The person shouldn't only be *talking*; the person should also be *producing*. What is going on inside should be apparent on the outside. When we choose a mentor, it's essential that we find out if that person has already gone where we want to go and already knows what we need to know. If that is not the case, we need to find another mentor.

It's great that when Mary showed up, something leaped inside of Elizabeth. As soon as she heard Mary's voice, there was a response of joy and excitement within her. Similarly, we also need to be hanging out with people who can get excited about what God is doing in our lives. What was in Mary was greater than what was in Elizabeth, but Elizabeth could still be happy and genuinely thrilled over what was happening in this young woman who had come to her for support. We all know people who can rejoice with us as long as what we have is less than theirs, older than theirs, cheaper than theirs, or smaller than theirs. As long as our job is less than theirs, our house older than theirs, our car cheaper than theirs, and our bank account smaller than theirs, they are right there cheering us on. But if we begin to prosper and get some things that are greater, newer, more expensive and bigger than what they already have, they become different people—envious and jealous of our newfound fortune. They become our haters instead of our helpers.

THE LOVE OF MOTHER AND SON

Life is hard for single parents, and times can get very rough. But God offers Mary as an example to encourage them. It started off rough, but she gave birth to Greatness. It started off with her being turned away, but it turned into triumph. It started off as a struggle, but turned into success. It started off with people putting her down, but it ended with God raising her child up. Jesus cherished His mother. We can only imagine the night Jesus was born—not in a palace, but in a stable. We can imagine Mary saying to Baby Jesus, "I'm sorry, my little one. I know who You are. I know You are destined for greatness. I'm sorry for bringing You into this world in a dirty stable. This isn't where You belong, but it's all that we can provide right now. I promise You, though, that I will always give You the best I can. And someday, Your Father will give You all the things I can't. But I love You, my baby. You are precious to me, and I will always be here for You. I am so thankful to God for You. You are beautiful. And someday, everyone will know who You are. But until then, know that I am here for You. You were in my womb, but now You are in my heart, and You will always be there. I love You so much."

When He was going through the most difficult moment of His life, dying on the cross for our salvation, Mary was there. Most people had forsaken Him, but Mary remained as close as she could to Him. Jesus looked down from the cross and saw her sorrow. John 19:26-27 tells us: "When Jesus saw his mother there, and the disciple whom he loved standing nearby, he said to her, 'Woman. here is your son,' and to the disciple, 'Here is your mother.' From that time on, this disciple took her into his home." Mary had watched out for Jesus, and now Jesus was watching out for Mary.

JESUS, THE STEPSON

Jesus' mother was initially a single parent, so He can understand what other single parents are going through. Mary and Joseph had other children together, but Jesus was the child who was different. Like His siblings, Mary was His mother; but unlike them, Joseph was not His father. He understands what it means to be the one in the family who is different. He understands what it means to live with a stepfather.

There's an incident recorded for us in Luke 2 about the time when Jesus, His parents, and other relatives and friends journeyed to Jerusalem for the Passover feast. When the festival ended and the whole group headed home, Joseph and Mary didn't realize Jesus wasn't with them until the end of their first day of travel, when they began asking the others if Jesus was with them and learned that He wasn't. It took them three whole days to find Him back in Jerusalem. To their amazement, He was in the temple courts, where the adult teachers were there asking Him questions. Everyone was astonished at what He knew and with what authority He spoke to them.

Luke 2:48-49 says, "When his parents saw him, they were astonished. His mother said to him, 'Son, why have you treated us like this? Your father and I have been anxiously searching for you.' 'Why were you searching for me?' he asked. 'Didn't you know I had to be in my Father's house?'"

On the surface, that may have sounded like a disrespectful response, like a slap in the face to His stepfather. It could have been interpreted as Jesus saying to Joseph, "*You* aren't my daddy. You can't tell me what to do." But the next verse makes it clear that was not the case. Verse 51 says, "Then he went down to Nazareth with them and was obedient to them." Jesus may have been only twelve, but He had enough sense to know that this man was worthy of His respect. This man loved His mother, accepted Him as his own son, and cared deeply about both of them. He provided for them, protected them, and loved them. Jesus knew that He was blessed to have him in His life, and He obeyed Joseph and His mother.

SOMEDAY IS COMING

In John 2 we read about another incident when Jesus was thirty years old. Mary, Jesus, and His disciples were invited to a wedding in Cana. We don't know if this was a relative getting married or if

Mary was a close friend of the hosts of the party, but for whatever reason, Mary noticed that they had run out of wine in the midst of this occasion. She mentioned this to Jesus, but she wasn't telling Him just as a matter of information. She was expecting Jesus to do something about it. She knew Him well enough to know that in one way or another, He could handle this. So she said to the servants in reference to Jesus, "Do whatever he tells you" (John 2:5). Jesus ordered them to fill six huge water jars with water, and then He turned it all into wine—better wine than the best that had already been served.

Can you imagine how that made Mary feel? After all of these years, people in their village still talked about her. They gossiped about the fact that she and Joseph got married early and that it was obvious that she was pregnant at that time. Some still called her and Jesus derogatory names. Mark 6:3 reveals that people didn't refer to Jesus as "Joseph's son," as He ordinarily would have been called during that time. Instead, they asked, "Isn't this Mary's son?" So, all of Jesus' life, He and Mary lived under the stigma of her unwed-mother status.

But *today* was different. *Today*, Mary's community needed *her*. *Today*, Mary was able to say, "My son can handle this. My son's got this thing. Just do what He tells you to do and watch what happens." All that she knew Him to be became evident that day to others. Who else's son could turn water into wine? Jesus performed His first miraculous sign at His mother's request. She was too humble a woman to say to others, "See, I told you so." But her son's actions spoke for both of them.

Single parents need to remember this lesson during the hard times: Things may be hard now, but someday they will be able to look at what their child is doing and say in their hearts, "See, I told you so." Things may be hard now, but someday the same people who called them and their baby ugly names will be coming to them and asking for help. Things may be hard now, but someday all the amazing things they know to be true about their child will be revealed to others. Things may be hard now, but "someday" is coming!

BE WILLING TO CHANGE PLANES

I had just returned from a trip to Haiti. When I flew back to the States from Port-au-Prince, I flew into Miami, where I had a six-hour layover for my connecting flight to Indianapolis. I wasn't upset. I was working on a sermon, so I used the time to finish that. I wasn't anxious or angry. It was all okay. When I arrived in Miami, it was about noon. Now it was about 6:45 p.m. and time for me to get on the plane to come home. I had to speak to the ministers in my church at eight o'clock the next morning, but I thought, "This is okay. I'll get home in time to get a good night's sleep to be ready for that meeting." So I boarded the plane, and we took off for Indianapolis, my destination.

About thirty minutes into the flight, however, the pilot announced over the PA system, "I'm sorry to have to tell you this, but we have to return to the Miami airport. There is mechanical difficulty: the flap on one of the wings doesn't work. We are supposed to fly at 37,000 feet, but because of the broken flap, we are only able to maintain an altitude of 27,000 feet. We are burning more fuel than we would need to burn, so we have to go back to have it repaired."

Trying to calm and comfort us, he assured us that he would get us to our destination. He said, "Our plan is to repair the plane. But if that doesn't work out, we have other planes that will take you to your destination."

We went back to the airport. They tried to fix the plane, but that didn't work, so they put us on another plane to get us to our destination. Now, it would have been foolish for us to try to get to our destination in a plane that was flying too low and using far too much energy. So, instead of being foolish, we got off of something that couldn't be repaired and got on to something that could get us where we needed to go.

If we are in relationships that are too lowdown, broken, and not going anywhere, we don't need to get angry or depressed. If God can't repair one relationship, He has others for us that will take us exactly where we need to be. Just be willing to change planes.

God,

We thank You that You desire good for us and not evil. Thank You that You love us even when we don't love ourselves. We need You today. We know that You want us to be happy with Plan B, but Plan A looked SO perfect. Help us to accept Plan B as Your will for our lives. Help us to see what You see and to be open to all that You have in store for us. Give us people to walk alongside us for a time and a purpose. And help us to be willing to change. Amen.

CHAPTER 5

A FULFILLED SINGLE PARENT: IT'S NOT TOO LATE

> Soon afterward Jesus went with his disciples to the village
> of Nain, and a large crowd followed him. A funeral pro-
> cession was coming out as he approached the village gate.
> The young man who had died was a widow's only son,
> and a large crowd from the village was with her. When
> the Lord saw her, his heart overflowed with compassion.
> "Don't cry!" he said. Then he walked over to the coffin
> and touched it, and the bearers stopped. "Young man," he
> said, "I tell you, get up." Then the dead boy sat up and
> began to talk! And Jesus gave him back to his mother.
>
> (Luke 7:11-15 NLT)

AIN'T DEAD YET

It was February 26, 2014. By nine o'clock that Wednesday night, Walter Williams' family had gathered in Lexington, Mississippi. Walter was having a bad night, and the family watched as he slipped away into death. A hospice nurse confirmed he was dead. His nephew was there, and he got on the phone and called the authorities. They showed up at the home, and everyone waited for the coroner to arrive. The coroner came, checked the body, and saw no signs of life. He checked for a pulse, and finding none, he officially declared Walter Williams dead.

The nephew stood by and watched as his uncle was put into a black body bag that they promptly zipped up. The body was taken to Porter & Sons Funeral Home. It lay there all of Wednesday night. On Thursday morning, Walter Williams' body was taken to the embalming room, where staff members were waiting to prepare it for burial. While they were setting up to do the embalming, the staff heard some noise coming from the body bag. The "late" Walter Williams was kicking, and it was obvious that he was breathing now as well. Naturally, the workers were shocked. They quickly unzipped the body bag and rushed him to the hospital, where he was treated and remained alive for about two more weeks—much to the joy and surprise of his family.

Of course, the question on everyone's lips was this: How did this happen? The authorities, the community, and the family all wanted to know how this man could have been declared dead when he was still alive. The coroner said that it was nothing short of a miracle, even though there was a valid explanation. He said that the pacemaker Mr. Williams wore must have somehow jump-started his heart some time after he was placed in the body bag—some time after everyone knew he had died. Whatever the reason for his resurrection, this was truly a miracle for the family. At 2:30 a.m. on Thursday, Mr. Williams' son called his cousin who had watched the man being zipped up in the body bag and said, "Not yet. Daddy's still here."

What I want single parents to know is that it's not too late. It doesn't matter how many people have said there is no future for your child. It doesn't matter how many people have said his or her life is as good as over. It doesn't matter how many people have said, "There's no hope." With Jesus Christ, it is still not too late.

WHEN IT'S OVER, IT'S OVER

In the Scripture passage for this chapter, we encounter a single mother who was facing a terrible situation. She had already lost her husband, and now she had lost her only son too. Jesus was making His way from Capernaum, a major city in Galilee where He had done many miracles and where five of His disciples had lived. If

Jesus had established a "headquarters" (a place where most of His work took place), it would have been Capernaum. The healing of the man whose friends lowered him down through the roof to Jesus happened in Capernaum. The healing of Peter's mother-in-law from her fever took place in Capernaum. It was also in Capernaum that Jesus healed the centurion's servant—not by going to his house, but simply by speaking the word of healing for that man. Jesus praised the faith of the centurion, a man who held a high political and social position in Capernaum.

When Jesus left Capernaum to go to Nain, He was leaving a place of popularity to go to a place of obscurity. He was not encountering a man at a high level on the ladder of economic and social status, but reaching down to a woman who was at the bottom of that ladder. A single woman had no esteem within her community, and she certainly had no economic security. But that didn't matter to Jesus. Someone can be at the top or the bottom of a socioeconomic ladder, and that makes no difference to Him. This is an important point for single parents to notice. It doesn't matter whether others have praised them or dismissed them, Jesus is still there for them. When we get to the point that we no longer care so much about how others see us and we gain the assurance of how Jesus sees us, then we have the confidence that everything is going to be alright.

Jesus went to a place of obscurity, a place off the beaten path, so to speak. He went to a woman whose husband had died, and now her only son had died as well. Her situation reflected both her relationships and resources. She had a dead relationship with her son's father. He was dead and never coming back. With her son's father, there could never be a reconnection, a reconciliation, or a restoration. That man could not help her pay her bills, pay her rent, or buy those things she needed. He could not be there to support her in this time of emotional upheaval. He was not coming back. That relationship was over. She had to come to the acceptance that it was dead.

The bad news for some single mothers is that their baby's daddy is not coming back. The bad news for some single fathers is that their baby's mama is not coming back. It is very sad. It is not what we wish were true. It is a bitter pill to swallow. This is a relationship issue and the relationship, however it dissolved, is over. The relationship is dead.

But truly accepting that bad news is the first step to receiving God's good news. Acknowledging that the relationship is dead frees us to be open to something new, something that is alive, something that God has in store.

DEATH AND DEPLETION

The widow faced not only a relationship issue, but also a resource issue. Women in Galilee at this point in time got their identity and resources through the men in their lives. A woman was somebody's daughter, then somebody's wife, and then somebody's mother. Her value came from her men. This was a male-dominated society, and women were treated as property.

This widow had value when her husband was alive. He put a roof over her head and took care of her and their children. She could be proud because she was the wife of so-and-so. She had her needs met because her husband met those needs. Even when her husband died, she still had value because she was the mother of a son. Children started working then at a young age, so she could count on her son for income. Her future was still secure because she had a son who would take care of her. But now, her value, her income, and her hopes for the future were all gone because her son was gone.

I want to stop here to remind all of us that we do not live in the first century. Nor do we live in Capernaum or Nain. We live in the twenty-first century in the United States of America. Women do not have to wait for a man to bring them value. They don't have to wait for a man for confirmation, affirmation, or identification. All of that comes to a woman through her relationship with Jesus Christ. When she accepts Jesus as her Savior, she becomes a child of the King. A woman who is the child of a king is a princess. She does not need to wait for a man to bring her value or valuables.

In twenty-first century America, a woman can go to school for herself, get her own degree, make her own money, buy her own house, purchase her own car, pay for her own clothes and meet all of her own needs. A woman in a relationship with Jesus Christ can accomplish all that God has in store to give her an abundant life.

FOLLOWING HIS FATHER'S FOOTSTEPS

For the widow in the Luke account, it was about depleted resources as well as dead relationships. After seeing that her husband died before his son was grown, the widow had undoubtedly hoped that their son would not follow in his father's footsteps. She had hoped in her heart that what had happened to her husband would not happen to their son. She wanted her son to grow old and see his children and his grandchildren. But now, her son had died earlier even than his father did.

There was a proverb quoted in Old Testament times that was referenced in Ezekiel 18:2: "The fathers eat sour grapes, and the children's teeth are set on edge." This meant that if the fathers did something they shouldn't do, their children also would reap the bitter consequences of their actions. E. K. Bailey interpreted this by saying, "The sins of the fathers frustrate their children." Dr. Kenneth Ulmer, pastor of Faithful Central Bible Church in Inglewood, California, says, "The traits of the fathers become the tendencies of the children." Rev. Freddie Haynes says, "The habits of fathers become the hang-ups of the children." Even if our children never commit the sins that we commit, they will still struggle with them. There is a predisposition in our children because of the sins we commit.

There is an argument even today among sociologists, psychologists, theologians, and others about whether this tendency of the children to follow in their father's footsteps is genetic or environmental. When we have a predisposition for the same choices, habits, and behaviors as our parents, does that come from our genetic make-up? Do our genes determine our behavioral propensities in the same way they determine our hair color, eye color, and other physical attributes? Or do we often take on the behaviors and attitudes of our parents simply because we live with them and their behaviors and attitudes rub off on us over time?

NOT ENVIRONMENT OR GENETICS, BUT JESUS

As I told the single parents with whom I met, my father's departure from our family when I was eight years old was both a blessing and a curse. It was the best thing that could have happened to me at that young age, and the worst thing that could have happened. It was the worst thing that could have happened because I needed my father. Children need their fathers in their lives. My subsequent behavioral and emotional issues were evidence of the absence of my father from my life.

But my father leaving our home was also the best thing that could have happened. That may sound strange, but since he left when I was eight, that meant I spent less time in the environment he created. I had to spend only eight years around someone who was drinking, smoking, gambling, swearing, committing adultery, and not caring for his family as he should have. Had he lived with us longer, those behaviors would have had a greater chance of becoming part of what I would view as normal.

Those of us who grow up in that sort of environment often promise ourselves, "I'm not going to be like my father." But what happens in actuality is that we become just like the person we said we were not going to be like. So do we become like our parents because of our environment, or genetics?

This great debate will undoubtedly continue, but the good news is that when we give our lives to Jesus, all of that can change. Second Corinthians 5:17 says, "Therefore, if anyone is in Christ, the new creation has come: The old has gone, the new is here!" That is the reason why, in spite of the genes I inherited from my father and the environment he created for me, I am able to follow Jesus and do what God wants me to do with my life. This includes loving my wife, caring for my children, and being a positive member of my community. My behavior and attitudes are no longer determined by my earthly father, but by my heavenly Father. First John 3:9 tells us that when we are born again, God's seed remains in us. So now I have a predisposition towards my heavenly Father. I can make the decisions that He would make because His seed is in me.

Single parents do not need to focus on the bad traits their children may have received from their father or their mother. Instead, they need to help their children get to know Jesus and be adopted into God's family so that they are now influenced by Him and by His characteristics.

One of the words we use for "salvation" is "regeneration." The base word in "regeneration" is "gene." When we get saved, God essentially "re-genes" us so we don't have to live according to the negative genes of our parents. Now we can live according to the holy, righteous genes of our heavenly Father. Receiving Christ as our Savior and having God as our heavenly Father makes a difference in how we live.

WHEN JESUS SHOWS UP

The widow's son was dead. Some of our children today are not dead physically, but they are dead spiritually. In Ephesians 2:1, Paul uses the phrase, "you were dead in your transgressions and sins." Spiritual death involves our separation from God.

It's obvious when someone is dead because that person is immobile and insensitive. It was very apparent that the widow's son was dead because he didn't even respond to the tears of his mother. If a child doesn't respond when his or her mother is crying, it's obvious that child is dead. If our mother's tears don't prompt a response from us, we must have died in some way. There are many parents today who can't understand why their children don't respond to them, why they don't care about them, why they don't appreciate anything they do, and why they can even see that they are hurting yet not feel something inside. These parents don't understand that their children have died.

These parents don't understand why their children aren't moved by the things of God, why they aren't moved when they hear the Word of God preached, and why they don't respond to God's voice speaking to their hearts. These parents don't understand that their children have died.

But it was only when the widow's child had died that Jesus showed up. And that is good news for parents today. The same Jesus who cared about that single mother and her child cares about us today and our children. It doesn't matter how unmoved the child has become. It doesn't matter how unfeeling that child is. It doesn't matter that others have pronounced the child dead. Nothing else matters when Jesus shows up.

Jesus shows up in our circumstances even in obscure places, even if others are looking down on us, and even if others devalue us. And Jesus shows up at just the right time. Just when we need Him most, Jesus comes on the scene. It is not too late. No matter what the circumstances, it is not too late for Jesus to come and change the situation.

History illustrates for us that Jesus will show up. Shadrach, Meshach and Abednego were thrown into a fiery furnace, but when Nebuchadnezzar looked into that furnace, he saw *four* persons there. He said, "And the form of the fourth is like the Son of God" (Daniel 3:25 KJV). Jesus showed up!

At the pool of Bethesda, there was a man who had suffered as an invalid for thirty-eight years. He lay there among the blind, the lame, and the paralyzed, hoping for a miracle. One day, Someone told him to do the impossible, to take up his mat and walk—and he did. Jesus showed up!

One day in Jericho, a blind man named Bartimaeus was sitting beside the road, begging. He called out so loudly that others told him to be quiet. But he kept yelling, "Son of David, have mercy on me." He came to Jesus, and his faith enabled him to see again. He was a poor, blind beggar, but Jesus showed up!

Once there was a man in the synagogue with a shriveled hand. In spite of his pain, discomfort, and perhaps even embarrassment, he made his way to the place of worship. While spiritual leaders argued about the legality of healing on the Sabbath, this man's hand was healed because that day, Jesus showed up!

In Matthew 18:20, Jesus says, "For where two or three gather in my name, there am I with them." Jesus will show up! As truly as Jesus showed up for those people in the Bible who needed Him, He will show up in our lives too. And when Jesus shows up, compassion shows up, healing shows up, restoration shows up, grace shows up, mercy shows up, and power shows up. It's never too late for Jesus to show up.

DON'T CRY

In our Luke 7 account, the *New Living Translation* speaks of the boy lying in a coffin. Actually, in those days he would have merely been wrapped in grave clothes and laid out on a stretcher. Then his body would have been carried outside the city walls. The Jews would never bury their dead within the city limits. Jesus encountered the funeral procession as He was approaching the city gate and the procession was coming out.

When Jesus decided to intervene in the situation, He did not immediately approach the boy. Instead, He first spoke to the mother. The child was dead, and Jesus could see that. So He didn't speak to the dead child, but to the mother. What He said to the mother surprised me. He said, "Don't cry!" If any mother had a right to cry, this mother had a right to cry. Her man was dead, her son was dead, her resources were depleted, and she was on her way to the graveyard to bury her beloved boy. This woman had reason to cry. But Jesus walked up to her and said, "Don't cry."

How could Jesus tell her not to cry when He also cried at a funeral? According to John 11, we know that Jesus went to visit Lazarus' family after his friend died, and He wept. If He could cry at a friend's funeral, why would He tell this woman not to cry at her own son's funeral?

In over thirty years of officiating at funerals, I have *never* told anyone not to cry—especially not a family member. How could I show up as a pastor at a funeral and tell someone not to cry? That's absurd. That would be totally insensitive. Crying is an emotional release. It is therapeutic for people to cry when they are hurting deeply. God has given us tears for this life because Revelation 7:17 tells us of a time to come when "God will wipe away every tear from their eyes." So if tears are a gift from God, why would Jesus tell this woman not to cry?

Read His words again in context: "When the Lord saw her, his heart overflowed with compassion. 'Don't cry!' he said" (Luke

7:13 NLT). His words, "Don't cry," were not a heartless command. Instead, this was a loving response as "his heart overflowed with compassion" towards the woman. Think of a loving parent whose little daughter is heartbroken because her favorite doll got broken, or whose little boy fell and skinned his knee. When the parent says, "Don't cry," the words are spoken in this context: "Don't cry, honey. Come here and let me take care of it." Jesus' words were spoken in that same context.

Jesus said to the woman, "Don't cry," and then He immediately came into the situation to transform it. He began working to take away the very cause of her tears. He wants to do that even today for single parents. There are many single parents crying today because they hurt deeply over the condition of their children. Jesus is saying to them, "Don't cry. I'm here. Watch what I'm going to do."

WHAT DO WE REALLY WANT?

Crying in itself will not change our circumstances. Crying isn't going to bring back your man or your woman. Crying isn't going to bring back a wandering child. Crying isn't going to pay the bills or put money in your pocket. Crying isn't going to put your child through school. Crying is simply going to waste a lot of energy and effort that are needed to do something positive. There are times that Jesus tells us to stop crying, but He doesn't just say that and walk away. When He says that, it means He is coming closer—into our very situation. He is coming to transform our circumstances. He is coming to breathe life into something that was dead.

Jesus wants us to know that our crying accomplishes nothing in terms of bringing about a positive change. We are not rewarded on the basis of how hard or long we cry. He didn't want the widow woman to think that it was her crying that brought about the miracle she was about to experience. If she believed that, then the next time she was in trouble, she would simply sit down and cry. She wouldn't do anything that would bring about a change in her circumstances. That is *not* what God wants from us. In fact, some people become so overwhelmed emotionally that they actually miss the fact that God is already on the scene and ready to work in their lives.

Ecclesiastes 3:1 tells us, "There is a time for everything," and verse 4 continues, "a time to weep and a time to laugh, a time to mourn and a time to dance." Yes, there is a time to weep, and yes, there is a time to mourn, but there is also a time for our weeping to stop and our laughter to begin. There is a time when our mourning is supposed to stop and our dancing to begin again. Some people enjoy the weeping and the mourning too much. They get some sort of perverse compensation from their crying and complaining. Maybe they prefer being pitied over being prospered. Maybe they prefer the attention they get from their mourning more than the praise Jesus would get from His miracle. There is something wrong when someone would *rather* cry than sing.

Boyz II Men

When Jesus saw what was happening in the village of Nain, He walked over to the body of the young man who had died and spoke to him. Now, I personally believe that this young man died during the time of transition from childhood to young adulthood. I believe this mother lost her son during the transition between boyhood and manhood. Along with other theologians, based on the Greek word that was used, I believe this was a *young* man, an *immature* man, a youth who had not yet fully transitioned into manhood.

This passage can be confusing. In Luke 7:14, Jesus speaks to the "young man," but in verse 15, it says, "the boy" sat up and began to talk. So was this a young man, or was it a boy? I believe that he was both. He was in a period of transition from boyhood to manhood.

Sadly, it is during that period of transition that we lose so many of our children even today. Manhood is about maturity, responsibility, and spirituality. Before our boys reach manhood in terms of their level for these three areas, we lose them.

The reason we lose them is because of the crowd. In this passage from Luke 7, we see two crowds in the picture. There was one crowd who followed Jesus. Verse 11 says, "Soon afterward Jesus went with his disciples to the village of Nain, and a large crowd followed him." But they encountered another crowd in the village that was following the widow. Verse 12 says, "The young man who had died was a widow's only son, and a large crowd from the village was with her."

WHERE HAVE ALL OUR YOUNG MEN GONE?

If we look at the crowds in this story as an illustration, we could say that there was one crowd that didn't know what to do with a young man who was no longer able to see, hear, or experience emotions. They had no hope for him and felt that he would be of no use whatsoever to the community. So their way of handling such a young person was to put him away, take him out of the community, and move him to a place that they had prepared for him that was the same place they had taken his father a few years earlier.

In today's society, we have ways of dealing with young people who no longer function properly, who don't see as they should see, hear as they should hear, or feel towards others as they should feel. We put them away. We have places prepared for them away from the community; we have juvenile centers, jails, and prisons where we can send them—not to restore them, but to get rid of them.

But there is another crowd. Jesus is at the head of the other crowd. His solution is radically different. He, too, recognizes that the young people aren't seeing right, hearing right, or feeling emotions in a healthy way. But He doesn't want them to be put away. He wants to raise them up. This crowd that follows Jesus says, "We aren't about incarceration, but about restoration." This crowd doesn't want to bury the young people away, but to bring them back to life.

And there is always a third crowd made up of all the young people who are dead and dying, but haven't yet been either put away or restored. They can't hear, but they pretend they can. They can't see, but they pretend they can. They feel no compassion, no love, no sensitivity towards others, but they pretend they do. They say to an unsuspecting young person, "We care about you. Your family doesn't care. Your school doesn't care. This community doesn't care. But we're here for you. You follow us, and we've always got your back."

The problem is that when young people see crowds, they don't know how to distinguish one crowd from another. They see only what is on the surface, not what is real. They don't know that the crowd of pretenders really *can't* see as they see, hear as they hear, or feel as they feel. They take them at their word and don't find out until later that they can't see that they are headed towards a dead end.

They don't find out till later that this crowd can't hear all of the people calling to them—their parents, their teachers, their pastors, their neighbors, their youth leaders—telling them to turn around, to go another way in order to save their lives. Young people don't immediately understand that this crowd doesn't have natural human emotions. This crowd can see a child hurt and laugh about it; can beat and rob an elderly woman and somehow feel good about that. They can take a gun into a school and murder one person after another and feel like heroes. This crowd leads only to death and destruction, but sometimes young people become part of this crowd before they realize all of that. Then it's almost impossible for them to get out.

WHICH CROWD ARE WE IN?

There are always crowds around us throughout our lives. It is important for us to determine which crowd we will follow. As adults, we must choose whether we are going to be restorers or gravediggers. Are we going to bring misguided young people back to life or commit them to a hole just to get rid of them?

What type of a community are we helping to establish? Is it one of love and reconciliation, or one of hatred and isolation? Is it one in which we see all young people as our responsibility and reach out to help those in need? Or is it one in which we see some young people simply as an expendable commodity to be put away so we won't be bothered?

Jesus made it clear which crowd He leads. John 3:17 says, "For God did not send his Son into the world to condemn the world, but to save the world through him." And Jesus Himself said in John 10:10, "I have come that they may have life, and have it to the full." Jesus is always into life, redemption, and restoration.

Young men and young women—boys and girls who are in the process of transitioning into manhood and womanhood—often have difficulty choosing which crowd to follow. We as parents and other adults in their lives need to guide them toward choosing the right crowd. We don't want them to follow a crowd that will lead them to destruction. Nor do we want them to look around and find themselves surrounded by people who simply see them as problems to be dealt with, instead of beautiful human beings created by God for a purpose and a destiny.

We want them to be surrounded by people who are not blind to their faults and their flaws, but who can see beyond those to what God sees inside them. We want them to be surrounded by people who will lift them up, not put them down—people who will help them realize their potential, not quench the life that God has put within them.

CHILDREN NEED GUIDANCE

You may wonder how we as parents can help our children make the right decisions. There are so many ways. We do that by the choice of movies we watch, the websites we pull up, with our postings on Facebook, with the music we have playing in our home. With all of the choices we make, we are helping our children choose a crowd. By the people we invite into our home and the language and behavior we allow there, we are helping our children choose a crowd. By what we drink in the house and whether or not we smoke in the house, we are helping our children choose a crowd.

What is really interesting to me is that some parents think they are so educated and so sophisticated that they will not expose their children to the Jesus crowd while they are growing up. They have this erroneous idea that they can keep their children from knowing anything about Jesus all of their childhood and yet think that when they become adults "they can choose for themselves." How can they choose what they don't even know anything about?

There are a lot of wounded people in our churches. There are adults whose parents dragged them to church on Sundays during their childhood, but lived like the devil every other day of the week. As children, they observed that hypocrisy and wanted nothing to do with it. There are adults now whose parents were mean, bitter, and even abusive with them and who wrongly taught them that their strict discipline was part of being God-fearing people and doing things God's way. Of course, these children grew up determined to never be associated with a God like that. There are adults whose church, pastor, or Sunday school teacher abandoned them when they needed that person most, so they no longer have room in their lives for such people.

These adults have never found healing for themselves. They have never gotten to know Jesus as the One who has come to bring them life. They have never gotten to know God as their *loving* Father. They grew up with a false image of God and a misconception of what it means to be a Christian. So they leave God out of their homes and families and say that if their children want to choose that option when they are adults, they can do so. But who is going to let these children know who Jesus *really* is and what God is *really* like? Let's hope that the people in the crowd following Jesus will be so much like Him, others will be drawn to His love, kindness, and abundant life.

DECISION TIME

Some parents put on their church clothes on Sunday mornings and mingle with the Jesus crowd at church, but then they find the other crowd and hang with those folks the rest of the week. But we can't serve God like that. In fact, that isn't serving God at all. Those are two separate crowds going two completely opposite directions. In Matthew 7, Jesus acknowledged that His crowd is smaller. He said, "Wide is the gate and broad is the road that leads to destruction, and many enter through it. But small is the gate and narrow the road that leads to life, and only a few find it" (vv. 13-14). One crowd is bigger and easier to follow; the other is on a narrow road and has fewer people. But we have to make a decision. We can't follow both.

Moses made it clear to the people of Israel that they had a decision to make. Deuteronomy 30:15-18a records his declaration to them:

> See, I set before you today life and prosperity, death and destruction. For I command you today to love the LORD your God, to walk in obedience to him, and to keep his commands, decrees and laws; then you will live and

increase, and the LORD your God will bless you in the land you are entering to possess. But if your heart turns away and you are not obedient, and if you are drawn away to bow down to other gods and worship them, I declare to you this day that you will certainly be destroyed.

Then, in the next two verses, he called for them to make that decision: "This day . . . I have set before you life and death, blessings and curses. Now choose life, so that you and your children may live and that you may love the LORD your God, listen to his voice, and hold fast to him. For the LORD is your life."

Did you notice that he said, "that you *and your children* might live"? The decisions we make as parents have a direct effect upon our children. We are often not choosing just for ourselves, but for them as well. If we choose not to follow Jesus, not to make room in our lives for God, we are making the decision that Jesus will not be in their lives either.

In the Old Testament, Joshua recognized that the choice he made as a father was going to affect his entire family. He told the Israelites, "Now fear the LORD and serve him with all faithfulness . . . . But if serving the LORD seems undesirable to you, then choose for yourselves this day whom you will serve . . . . But as for me and my household, we will serve the LORD" (Joshua 24:14-15). He knew that he couldn't sit on the fence. He had to choose God or reject Him. And he knew that he was choosing not just for himself, but for his family too.

Recently on a TV show in which celebrities swap wives for a couple of weeks of platonic relationships with each other's families, a Jewish woman came to stay in the home of an avowed atheist. This man not only did not make room for God in his own life, but he ridiculed religious things in front of his children.

It was not too surprising, then, that as this Jewish woman was sincerely trying to let this family get to know her and what was important to her, they all mocked her faith. Even as she was lighting candles and reciting a blessing to usher in Shabbat (the Sabbath), the young children were openly laughing and poking fun at her, and their father took pride in their behavior. The children were ignorant;

they didn't know anything except what they had learned from their father. They were intolerant because he was intolerant. They saw religion as something to be laughed at because they were seeing it through his eyes. His choice was becoming their choice even though they had no idea they were making a choice.

JESUS SPOKE TO THE MAN

But in our Luke 7 account, Jesus knew that this young man was old enough to make decisions for himself. So, after Jesus spoke to his mother, He spoke directly to him. He didn't continue to talk to the mother; instead, He talked directly to the one who was dead. He said to the young man, "Get up!" (Luke 7:14). He didn't tell the mother to tell her son to get up. He knew it was time for the young man to do things for himself.

Some parents don't know when that time has come. Their son or daughter is in transition, but rather than speaking to the young man or woman they are *becoming*, they continue to speak to the boy or girl they have been. While allowing their adult children to live at home, the parents continue to buy their food, pay their expenses, and even give them spending money.

At some point, they need to stop speaking to the boy in the man and speak to the man in the boy. At some point, they need to stop speaking to the girl in the woman and speak to the woman in the girl. They need to say, "It's time now for you to be responsible for yourself. It's time for you to get a job, get your own place, and pay your own way. I'm not doing you any favors by treating you like a child. I need to treat you as an adult so that you will begin to treat yourself as an adult. I need to let you grow up so that you will, in fact, grow up. It's time."

POWER IN A WORD FROM THE LORD

It was when Jesus spoke to the man in the boy that he got up. Jesus knew he could do it because *He* had told him to get up. The young man couldn't have gotten up because of anything his mother, community, or friends said to him. They all said he was dead. But when *Jesus* tells us to do something, we can do it!

After Jesus' resurrection, but before He went to heaven, He appeared to some of His disciples one night. Peter told his friends he was going to go fishing, and they replied that they would join him. John 21:3b-6 tells the story:

> So they went out and got into the boat, but that night they caught nothing. Early in the morning, Jesus stood on the shore, but the disciples did not realize that it was Jesus. He called out to them, "Friends, haven't you any fish?" "No," they answered. He said, "Throw your net on the right side of the boat and you will find some." When they did, they were unable to haul the net in because of the large number of fish.

What they weren't able to do for themselves, they could do when *Jesus* told them to do it.

It is the word of the Lord that makes all the difference. We can work hard and long to try to accomplish something on our own, but end up with nothing. However, when we are obeying the word of the Lord, we will see the task accomplished. We can be facing an impossible situation, but when we act on the word of the Lord, the impossible becomes possible. We can be facing insurmountable obstacles, but when Jesus comes and speaks a word into our lives, either the obstacles disappear or God makes a way for us to get around them.

Some people get discouraged and depressed and think that their situation is hopeless, but that's because they haven't yet listened to the word of the Lord. They have listened to parents, their spouse, therapists, teachers, pastors, friends, Dr. Phil, and a host of others, but their circumstance remains the same. They need to stop and ask, "God, what do You say about this? What do You think I should do?" There is power in a word from God.

In Matthew 8, we learn of a centurion who knew that there was power in a word from God. Verses 5-10 and 13 tell the story:

When Jesus had entered Capernaum, a centurion came to him, asking for help. "Lord," he said, "my servant lies at home paralyzed, suffering terribly." Jesus said to him, "Shall I come and heal him?"

The centurion replied, "Lord, I do not deserve to have you come under my roof. But just say the word, and my servant will be healed. For I myself am a man under authority, with soldiers under me. I tell this one, 'Go,' and he goes; and that one, 'Come,' and he comes. I say to my servant, 'Do this,' and he does it."

When Jesus heard this, he was amazed and said to those following him, "Truly I tell you, I have not found anyone in Israel with such great faith.... Then Jesus said to the centurion, "Go! Let it be done just as you believed it would." And his servant was healed at that moment.

The centurion knew that Jesus didn't have to be there visibly for his servant to be healed. He knew that a word from Jesus carried power. He knew that if Jesus merely said the word, the servant would be healed. He knew that a word from Jesus represented Jesus' presence in the midst of the situation, and that whatever the word said, it would be done. It's high time for some of us to stop crying, complaining, cussing, pouting, and wallowing in self-pity. We need to apply the Word of God to our situations because there is power in the Word.

SOMETIMES A TOUCH ACCOMPANIES THE WORD

When we look at the Luke 7 story, we see that Jesus didn't yell to the young man from a distance. He could have. He healed the centurion's servant from a distance. There is power in His word. He could have just yelled out across the crowd, "Young man, get up!" And the boy would have heard and gotten up. But Jesus wanted to teach us something else from this encounter. He wanted to teach us the importance of sometimes touching the situation around us.

We can learn something from each incident in which Jesus brought someone back to life. Jesus once raised from the dead the daughter of Jairus, a synagogue leader. The little girl had died, and Luke 8:54-55 tells us, "But he [Jesus] took her by the hand and said, 'My child, get up!' Her spirit returned, and at once she stood up. Then Jesus told them to give her something to eat."

And the third time He raised someone from the dead, it was his friend Lazarus. According to John 11:43-44, "Jesus called in a loud voice, 'Lazarus, come out!' The dead man came out, his hands and feet wrapped with strips of linen, and a cloth around his face. Jesus said to them, 'Take off the grave clothes and let him go.' "

In the first situation, Jesus simply took the girl's hand and said, "My child, get up!" In the second scenario, Jesus called the dead to come out the tomb. From a distance, He called in a loud voice, "Lazarus, come out!" But this time, He touched the bier, the wooden structure that was carrying away the body of the dead young man. His touch stopped the pallbearers in their tracks, and then Jesus turned the situation around. Then Jesus told the young man to get up.

LETTING GOD WORK

Thankfully, when Jesus began to address the young man's situation, his mother didn't get in the way. She had already done everything she knew how to do. She watched over her son throughout his life. She cared for him anytime he got hurt or got sick. She made sure his needs were met, even if she had to sacrifice her own needs. She loved him and tried to help and guide him. She did all that a mother could do, yet still her son died.

Now, here was this Jesus coming along and stopping the funeral procession. She had no idea what He was up to, but she allowed Him to do what He wanted to do. When He touched the bier, she didn't tell Jesus to leave her son alone. She didn't lash out at Him and say, "If you wanted to do something to help, you should have come sooner. Just leave him alone and let me bury him." She didn't question Jesus: "Why are you talking to him? Don't you know he's dead? He can't hear you! He can't see you! He doesn't know you're here. Just go away! Who are you anyhow? What business is this of yours?" Instead, she allowed Jesus to work and saw a miracle happen.

We need to see more of the touch of Jesus in our own lives. We need Him to touch our home, our jobs, our families, our relationships, our friendships, our finances, our dreams, and every aspect of our lives. When we begin to see the hand of God in our lives, it is important that we allow Him to do all that He wants to do. We shouldn't question Him. We shouldn't argue with Him. We shouldn't doubt Him. We should stand aside and say, "Lord, I've done all that I could do and look at what a mess this is. Please touch my circumstances. Please bring life into this dead situation. Do whatever You need to do, but please help me."

When Jesus had raised the young man back to life, Luke 7:15 says, "He gave him back to his mother." He didn't tell him that it was time for him to make his way on his own without any help from his mother. Jesus understands that it is okay for a mother to help support her child during this time of transition. The boy still needs help, but the man needs to be free to mature and take on more responsibility as he grows older. The mother needs wisdom to know how to care for the boy's needs, and yet see and nurture the man within him. She needs to be able to let the boy decrease so that the man can increase. She cannot continue to see him as a child, or she will treat him as a child. She needs to see the man that he is becoming and then do those things that will nurture the growth of that man.

It's All About the Timing

I still have a seventeen-year-old at home. He is six-foot-five. Sometimes when I look at him, he looks like a boy. Some other times when I look at him, he looks like a man. He's not still a boy, but he's not yet a mature man. He is in transition. Sometimes he talks and sounds like a boy, but there are other times when he talks with the maturity of a grown man. Sometimes he plays with PlayStation like a boy, but other times, he says, "I have to go to work"—which is like a man. Sometimes he plays electronic games like a boy. At other times, he whispers on the phone to a girl like a man. It is during this transition period that his mother and I have to be careful. We have to speak to the man in the boy in order to nurture him to where he is supposed to be. When our children are in transition, we have to help them through it.

It seems to me that boys often go too slowly through the transition. There are too many boys in grown men's bodies who are still playing with toys and still playing games. They are still living at home. They are still depending on Mama and Daddy to take care of them. They let their mamas cook for them and do their laundry. They offer excuses instead of effort. They got stuck in their transition and never became the men they were destined to become. They have men's bodies, but they are still immature, selfish, lazy boys, and they don't even aspire to change. They have deceived themselves. They are living at their daddy's house, driving their mama's car, getting money from their girlfriend for gas, and then bragging, "I'm my own man." Yet a real man will handle his own business. He will take on his own responsibilities. He will care for his own spirituality.

Now, I don't have any daughters, but it has been my observation that girls often seem to want to rush things. They seem to want to move quickly from girlhood to womanhood. They want to start dating at twelve or thirteen. Some of them begin having sex at fourteen. Some of them are pregnant by age fifteen, having a second baby by age seventeen and can't even *spell* "husband," let alone get one. Young women who do this miss out on their girlhood.

They should be doing their homework in the evenings, not taking care of babies. They should be picking out what clothes they want to wear to school the next day, not washing baby clothes. They should be participating in extracurricular activities and having fun, not trying to find a job without a high school diploma and worrying about how they are going to pay for diapers and baby food. While they are still girls, they are too young to realize what they are doing to their lives. It is only as they truly begin to mature that they look back and see what they have missed, but by then it's too late. They can never go back and recapture that lost period of their lives.

There are some young people who know they've messed up. They know their lives are not what they should be. They know they're headed in the wrong direction, but don't know how to stop.

They look at their insurmountable issues and they say, "If Jesus really wants to help me, where is He? Why doesn't He come? It's going to be too late. Why isn't He here?"

But Jesus is never late. In fact, He is always right on time, just like when He performed this miracle in Nain. He used the restoration of this dead young man to speak to an entire community. Luke 7:16 and 17 (NLT) say, "Great fear swept the crowd, and they praised God, saying, 'A mighty prophet has risen among us,' and 'God has visited his people today.' And the news about Jesus spread throughout Judea and the surrounding countryside." Jesus wasn't too late. If Jesus had shown up earlier, the crowd would not have been there to see His miracle. Because others were there, news spread quickly about this Jesus, the "mighty prophet" who had walked there among the people.

Jesus' work didn't just involve raising this one young man and ministering to this one widow woman. It wasn't only about them. He wanted everyone around to know that He is one who cares about their deepest pain. Everyone else needed to know that this Jesus doesn't just talk, but He can actually make a difference in a situation. This Jesus can breathe life into one who is dead and can make a family whole again. Jesus came at just the right time to reach not just this one family, but to reach the entire community with the good news that He had come.

BLESSINGS IN THE STORMS

After ministering to a group of pastors on the East Coast, I had to fly back to Indianapolis through Washington, D. C., and I had to stay on schedule. When I received the invitation to speak to this group, I told them that the only way I would come there is if they could guarantee that I could get back home Saturday night so that I could be at my church to preach on Sunday morning. They had informed me that there was a flight from New York City that would connect me with another flight in Washington, D. C., in order to get home when I needed to be there. So I agreed to make the trip and flew out of New York City on time to make my connecting flight home.

What none of us could have known, however, is that Washington, D. C. was going to experience a blizzard that night. The storm covered the entire East Coast. Not only was my flight delayed, it was cancelled. Here I was, trying to get to my destination in order to do what I had been called to do, but despite all of my best efforts, the flight was cancelled.

I had two options. One of those involved my own attitude. I have learned over the years that contentment is a choice. Whether we are catching a bus or riding in a Bentley, it is still our choice to be content. When we are going through a difficult situation, we can become mean and bitter and treat others badly, or we can celebrate the fact that God is with us so that we won't go through the situation alone.

When I found myself in the storm, I had a choice to make. I could have gotten upset and started complaining and feeling sorry for myself: "Here I am a pastor, and all I want to do is get home to minister to my congregation but can't get there. Why did God allow this storm to come? I should never have agreed to speak to these ministers." My other option was to thank God that He was with me and would take care of my stormy situation. Neither attitude was going to change my circumstances; I was still going to be in the storm no matter how I responded to it. But one response would bring glory to God, and the other would not.

I called John Jenkins, a friend of mine who pastors the First Baptist Church of Glenarden, Maryland, one of the largest churches in America. We've been friends for years, so I felt comfortable calling him to ask for a favor. I explained to him that I was stranded right there in Washington. I asked him to send one of the men from his church to pick me up at the airport and take me to a hotel. Then I told him I wanted to attend his church tomorrow if that same person could pick me up at the hotel and take me to the church in the morning. John said, "I'm going to do better than that. I'm going to come and get you myself." I argued with him that since it was Saturday night, he needed to use that time to prepare his sermon for the next morning. But no matter how much I argued, he insisted, "No, I'm coming to get you myself."

Then he asked me, "Now, you know the Washington Wizards have a home game tonight. Would you like to go?"

"Are you kidding? Would I like to see John Wall and the Wizards play there on their home court?! Of course, I want to go to the game!"

Not only did we go to the game, but John Jenkins had tickets for seats in the third row, mid-court. I was sitting in a seat I never would have been in, enjoying something I never would have had the opportunity to enjoy, had it not been for the storm.

While we were watching the game, he asked me, "Jeffrey, do you want to preach for me in the morning?" (But I was hesitant, knowing how much his congregation loves him and that they come to hear *him* preach. A congregation doesn't grow to twenty thousand for no reason.)

"No, I don't want to preach for you," I replied. "I don't want people to be all angry with me because I'm preaching while you're sitting right there."

"It's not like that at all. My people like you."

"I like them, too, but I know they're coming to hear their own pastor," I countered.

Then he confided, "Man, I wasn't going to preach tomorrow anyway. I've had a crazy week and I'm just not up to it, so I'm glad the storm came and brought you here."

That next morning, I preached to more people in a church setting than I have ever preached to in that type of setting before. There were at least 10,000 people there. (Now, I've preached to more people than that in other types of venues, but never in one single church service.) And the only reason that I was there to share Jesus with that many people was because of the storm that I encountered. Had it not been for the storm, I wouldn't have been in the place I was in, preaching to all of those people about Jesus. God used that storm to direct my life and to get me to a place that I would never have gotten to on my own.

The storms that we go through are not intended to harm us, but to bless us. If we maintain an attitude of faith and trust during the storms, God will use those very circumstances to position us for blessing.

Lord,

Thank You that it is not too late. Thank You that all that You plan to do for us, You will do as we walk in your ways and follow Your Word. Help us to see our children as You see them—as the men and women they are meant to be. We thank You especially today, God, for the blessings in the storms. Thank You that what we are going through is not intended to harm us, but to bless us. Help us to declare Your faithfulness in the midst of the storm, not only after we have gotten through safely. We do have faith in You. We do trust You. We do look to You for all that we need. In Your holy name we pray, Amen.

CHAPTER 6

THE SINGLE PARENT:
FINDING YOUR PLACE

Then I witnessed in heaven an event of great significance. I saw a woman clothed with the sun, with the moon beneath her feet, and a crown of twelve stars on her head. She was pregnant, and she cried out because of her labor pains and the agony of giving birth. Then I witnessed in heaven another significant event. I saw a large red dragon with seven heads and ten horns, with seven crowns on his heads. His tail swept away one-third of the stars in the sky, and he threw them to the earth. He stood in front of the woman as she was about to give birth, ready to devour her baby as soon as it was born. She gave birth to a son who was to rule all nations with an iron rod. And her child was snatched away from the dragon and was caught up to God and to his throne. And the woman fled into the wilderness, where God had prepared a place to care for her for 1,260 days.

(Revelation 12:1-6, *NLT*)

JESUS AND THE LAST DAYS

The woman in this passage is the final single parent referred to in the Bible. From this portion of Scripture, we will learn that God has a place for single parents. If you are a single parent, you can find your place. The beloved disciple, John, wrote the book

153

of Revelation while he was in exile on the island of Patmos. As it tells us in Revelation 1:1-2 (NLT): "This is a revelation from Jesus Christ, which God gave him to show his servants the events that must soon take place. He sent an angel to present this revelation to his servant John, who faithfully reported everything he saw. This is his report of the word of God and the testimony of Jesus Christ."

In Revelation 12, John describes the terrible period in the future called "The Great Tribulation." This is a seven-year timeframe in which the Bible says that God is going to pour out His final judgments during a time referred to as the "eschaton" or "the last days." The Great Tribulation is different from the times of tribulation that we all face as we go through life. This is a time when God is going to pour out horrific judgment on humanity because of our rejection of Jesus Christ.

Some people believe that we are living in those days now, but I disagree. I don't think that the tribulations we are experiencing now even remotely compare to the extreme proportion of judgment that God will pour out during that seven-year period. I do, however, believe that we are indeed living in the last days, so we all need to get our relationship right with Jesus.

At the point we encounter John's vision in Revelation 12, the earth is about halfway through the Great Tribulation. In verse 1, John says, "Then I witnessed in heaven an event of great significance." He goes on to talk about the pregnant woman that he sees. Some biblical scholars think this pregnant woman refers to Israel. They believe this because Jesus came through the Jewish lineage. Other theologians think that the pregnant woman represents the church. Either way, we do know that Jesus was born through the Virgin Mary. God's Holy Spirit overshadowed Mary, and she became impregnated with God's Son.

The child to whom she gives birth in verse 5, "will rule all nations with an iron rod." We know that this child is Jesus. Psalm 2 speaks about how God has placed His Son, his Anointed One, on the throne to be His Chosen King. And Psalm 2:9 specifically mentions the "iron rod" that Jesus will use to smash the enemies who rise up against Him. There is no doubt that the son in Revelation 12 is Jesus.

THE BATTLE BEGINS IN THE WOMB

When Mary became pregnant with God's Son, she was a virgin. So when we believe that life starts at conception (not at birth), we see Mary as a single parent. Parenthood starts when life starts. That's why women are always encouraged to get prenatal care for the health of the baby. That's also why women become protective of the baby within them.

It's amazing how quickly most mothers bond with their baby while that child is still in the womb. They are very much aware of the presence of a life growing within, a little one to love and cherish. They dream about what that baby might look like and what his or her personality might be like. They think about the name they want to give their baby—that distinct moniker by which their child will be known throughout his or her lifetime. Pregnant women can often be seen with their hands on their belly, gently rubbing that area to show love and comfort to the baby growing inside. Yes, parenthood definitely begins at conception.

In Revelation 12, after telling us that he saw this woman crying out as she was giving birth, John said that he saw a second significant event involving a red dragon. Verse 9 makes it clear that this great dragon was none other than "the ancient serpent called the devil, or Satan." Revelation 12:4 says that this evil one "stood in front of the woman as she was about to give birth, ready to devour her baby as soon as it was born."

Single parents need to understand that the moment they give birth, they enter into battle. It's a battle to raise children—to feed, provide shelter, and educate them. It's a battle to instill morals and values within children and protect them. It's a battle to lead children to Jesus, keep the world from luring them into an unhealthy lifestyle, and prevent the enemy from destroying their lives with drugs, alcohol, and all that is opposed to Jesus.

We shouldn't be surprised by the battles because as Christians we are in the midst of spiritual warfare. Ephesians 6:11-12 (NLT) cautions us, "Put on all of God's armor so that you will be able to stand firm against all strategies of the devil. For we are not fighting against flesh-and-blood enemies, but against evil rulers and authorities of the unseen world, against mighty powers in this dark world, and against evil spirits in the heavenly places."

We need to be watchful about how serious these battles are. The enemy isn't trying to embarrass us as parents or to simply make us look bad. No, the enemy is trying to destroy our children! We only have to watch a news report on TV, read a local newspaper, or listen to the news on the radio in order to hear about children being destroyed. Some of us can look around our neighborhoods and see that happening firsthand. Tragically, some of us have experienced that even in our own homes.

The enemy doesn't wait until a child becomes an adult, a teenager, or even an adolescent. Instead, he begins planning a child's destruction as soon as it is born. The enemy tried to get rid of Moses when he was just a baby because he didn't want Moses to grow up to deliver the Israelites from the land of Egypt. The enemy tried to kill Jesus as soon as the star appeared in the East to herald His birth because he didn't want Jesus to grow up, die on the cross, and be resurrected to become our Savior. The enemy comes early for our children because he knows that God has a plan and destiny for them to fulfill.

If the enemy comes for our children as soon as they are born, then we have to start the battle even before they are born. We have to make sure that we get the prenatal care that the baby needs to grow strong and healthy in the womb. We have to prepare a home for our child and arrange our lives so that he or she is coming into a loving, welcoming place. We can't learn to engage in spiritual warfare overnight, so we must not wait until the baby comes before we get our lives right with Jesus, begin praying for that child, join a church and become part of a positive community, or begin to make ourselves into the best parents we can possibly become. That needs to start early, while the baby is still safe within the mother's womb.

Biblical Symbolism

The Bible uses a lot of symbolism to convey significant concepts and principles. Biblical writers, for example, used the number seven to symbolize completion. Seven days *complete* a week. God rested on the seventh day because his work of creation was *completed*. The word "seven" and words stemming from that, such as "seventy," appear over five hundred times in the Bible.

The number ten is often used in the Bible to mean "whole." The *whole* law was summed up in the *Ten* Commandments. The *tenth* of our income that we give as a tithe is representative of the *whole* income God has given us. There were *ten* lepers made *whole* in Luke 17:11-17. In Luke 15:8-10, the woman scoured her house looking for one coin because it restored her *whole* amount of *ten*.

When the enemy is described in Revelation 12:3, he is depicted as one with great power. He appears as a dragon with seven heads, ten horns, and seven crowns. *Horns* represent power and *crowns* symbolize authority. Even as God is completely holy, the enemy is wholly evil. There is no evil within a holy God. There is no holiness in the evil one.

It seems to me that the enemy is getting both stranger and stronger. When we first met him in Genesis 3:1, he was a serpent. He was trying to deceive Adam and Eve, working on deceiving their minds. When we encountered him again in 1 Peter 5:8, he was a lion, "seeking whom he may devour." Now that we see him in Revelation 12, he is a large red dragon. And now he is not only out to destroy us, but to destroy our children. Stranger and stronger.

DECEPTION ABOUNDS

When we are faced with a battle, we have to choose sides. We can't sit on the sidelines and pretend to be neutral. In the spiritual battles we face, we are either on God's side or the devil's. We aim for heaven or hell. We *have* to choose a side. If we choose God's side, then we should be following Him. We should be guided according to His thoughts, led according to His direction, and living according to His ways. We are fighting for our children, so we have to side with the One who loves them and has a destiny for them.

We must remember that the enemy is very persuasive. That's why we have to monitor the things to which our children are exposed. We can't let them watch sin and degradation on TV shows and expect them to live holy and godly lives. We can't let them listen to music that leads them away from God and expect them to get close to Him. We can't let them look at pornography online and expect them to see others from God's perspective. We can't allow people in our homes who will entice them with the things of the world and then expect them to choose the things of God.

The Bible is filled with stories of deception and warnings against being deceived. These are only a few of the many examples of deception in the Bible:

- Then the Lord God said to the woman, "What is this you have done?" The woman said, "The serpent **deceived** me, and I ate" (Genesis 3:13).

- When morning came, there was Leah! So Jacob said to Laban, "What is this you have done to me? I served you for Rachel, didn't I? Why have you **deceived** me?"(Genesis 29:25).

- Then Laban said to Jacob, "What have you done? You've **deceived** me, and you've carried off my daughters like captives in war (Genesis 31:26).

- Then Joshua summoned the Gibeonites and said, "Why did you **deceive** us by saying, 'We live a long way from you,' while actually you live near us?" (Joshua 9:22).

- "You know Abner son of Ner; he came to **deceive** you and observe your movements and find out everything you are doing" (2 Samuel 3:25).

- "Ephraim is like a dove, easily **deceived** and senseless— now calling to Egypt, now turning to Assyria" (Hosea 7:11).

- The pride of your heart has **deceived** you, you who live in the clefts of the rocks and make your home on the heights, you who say to yourself, "Who can bring me down to the ground?" (Obadiah 1:3).

DON'T FALL FOR A FAKE

The deception does not come without God's faithful admonitions warning us not to be deceived. The Bible not only warns us not to allow others to deceive us, but also that we do not deceive ourselves. The following are only a few of God's words of counsel to us:

- Let him not **deceive** himself by trusting what is worthless, for he will get nothing in return (Job 15:31).

- An honest witness does not **deceive**, but a false witness pours out lies (Proverbs 14:5).

- Friend **deceives** friend, and no one speaks the truth. They have taught their tongues to lie; they weary themselves with sinning (Jeremiah 9:5).

- Yes, this is what the Lord Almighty, the God of Israel, says: "Do not let the prophets and diviners among you **deceive** you. Do not listen to the dreams you encourage them to have" (Jeremiah 29:8).

- Jesus answered: "Watch out that no one **deceives** you. For many will come in my name, claiming, 'I am the Messiah,' and will deceive many" (Matthew 24:4-5).

- For such people are not serving our Lord Christ, but their own appetites. By smooth talk and flattery they **deceive** the minds of naive people (Romans 16:18).

- Do not **deceive** yourselves. If any of you think you are wise by the standards of this age, you should become "fools" so that you may become wise (1 Corinthians 3:18).

- If anyone thinks they are something when they are not, they **deceive** themselves (Galatians 6:3).

- Let no one **deceive** you with empty words, for because of such things God's wrath comes on those who are disobedient (Ephesians 5:6).

- In fact, everyone who wants to live a godly life in Christ Jesus will be persecuted, while evildoers and impostors will go from bad to worse, **deceiving** and being **deceived** (2 Timothy 3:12-13).

- Don't be **deceived**, my dear brothers and sisters (James 1:16).

- If we claim to be without sin, we **deceive** ourselves and the truth is not in us (1 John 1:8).

In Matthew 24:24, Jesus warned, "For false messiahs and false prophets will appear and perform great signs and wonders to deceive, if possible, even the elect." If even the "elect" (those who know God and are close followers of God) are tempted to be deceived, how much more our children! They have come into the world and are trying to figure everything out—right from wrong, those they can trust from those they can't, whose voice to listen to and whose to ignore. There are so many demands for their attention, so they need their parents to run interference for them while they are too young to discern those who care and those who will do them harm.

GOD WINS

Revelation 12:4 says of the dragon, "Its tail swept a third of the stars out of the sky and flung them to the earth." This dragon is powerful. We cannot minimize or underestimate his power in this world. Revelation 12:9 refers to him as "that ancient serpent called the devil, or Satan, who leads the whole world astray." If he has the power to lead the whole world astray, that is *some* power!

But thank God, there is another power at work. Revelation 12:7-9 tells us what the angels of God were able to accomplish: "Then war broke out in heaven. Michael and his angels fought against the dragon, and the dragon and his angels fought back. But he was not strong enough, and they lost their place in heaven. The great dragon was hurled down . . . . He was hurled to the earth, and his angels with him."

Yes, the devil had angels working with him, too. You see, when God created this being called "the devil," he wasn't a devil then. Originally, he was an angel. His name was Lucifer. He did what some of us still do today. He exalted himself and tried to usurp the authority of God and place himself above God. He misused his freedom and became devilish. He began his work of deception and persuaded other angels to follow him instead of following God. But when he turned against God, God's forces turned against him. Isaiah 14:12-15 recorded what happened:

> How you have fallen from heaven,
>> morning star, son of the dawn!
> You have been cast down to the earth,
>> you who once laid low the nations!
> You said in your heart,
>> "I will ascend to the heavens;
> I will raise my throne
>> above the stars of God;
> I will sit enthroned on the mount of assembly,
>> on the utmost heights of Mount Zaphon.
> I will ascend above the tops of the clouds;
>> I will make myself like the Most High."
> But you are brought down to the realm of the dead,
>> to the depths of the pit.

We know the outcome of the story. We know that Jesus defeated the devil when He went to the cross. Jesus is able to protect those who are His. He is able to keep on the right track those who follow Him. And someday, there will be no more enemy. When the devil is thrown forever into the "lake of burning sulfur" (Revelation 20:10), we will no longer be in the battle that we are in today. There is a day coming when ALL will acknowledge that Jesus alone is King of kings and Lord of lords.

MORE THAN ONE LOOK

But until that day, we must "be alert and of sober mind, [because] your enemy the devil prowls around like a roaring lion looking for someone to devour" (1 Peter 5:8). Since the dragon has seven heads, that means there are at least seven faces that the devil wears.

Some people think they have the devil figured out and know what he looks like. But they don't realize that he takes on more than one disguise. Sometimes he can look mean and menacing to frighten us into doing what he wants us to do. But other times, he can look charming and engaging to draw us to himself so that we will be under his spell before we even know it. At other times, he can appear with his pockets full of good things that we need, and his face smiles as he promises to give us money, power, or whatever we need at that moment. Sometimes he will appear as a friend and draw us into a relationship that will ultimately destroy us. Sometimes he will appear as a wise leader—a pastor, teacher, or counselor—someone we *think* we can trust to give us wise advice and lead us in the right paths, only to dupe us and lead us away from God.

Remember that there are *at least* seven faces the devil can use to disguise his true self and his true motives. When even mature adults can be fooled, how can a child discern between the faces of good and evil? A child can't. That's why it is critical for parents to discern for them and to make sure there isn't a devil hiding in the midst of the child's acquaintances.

I think LeBron James is a great basketball player. But I'm not the only one who thinks he is amazing; every coach whose team he plays against thinks that. Every team that comes against LeBron James has a strategy not simply to defeat the team, but one to defeat James himself. The reason is that they believe if they can stop LeBron James, they will automatically be able to stop the team.

I've watched how they try to stop him: They present themselves to him with more than one look. It won't be the same person guarding him throughout the game. They know how productive he is, so they present more than one "look," more than one person, to try to stop him. They may start the game with a six-foot-eight guard weighing two hundred and fifty pounds. They think they will use that power to try to bang him at the beginning of the game. But then LeBron steps out and starts shooting three-pointers.

Recognizing that the first face wasn't thwarting him, they send in another. This person is six-foot-nine with long arms that he keeps flailing in front of LeBron to try to get him off his game. But LeBron just drives around him as though he isn't there. So, after another time-out, LeBron sees that he is looking at yet another face. This person is six-foot-two and can move really quickly, so he thinks he can outmaneuver LeBron, who is taller and a little heavier. But LeBron just backs him down and shoots over him.

So then the other team brings in some guy who hasn't yet proved he even belongs in this league. The team knows that this guy is no match for LeBron James, but he comes in the game with six fouls at his disposal. He is instructed simply to use all of his six fouls on LeBron James. He may not be able to outplay this amazing athlete, but he can impede his game and keep him distracted. So to help lead his team to victory, LeBron James has to face one adversarial look after another and overcome them all. No matter what he faces, however, he still averages twenty-eight points, seven rebounds, and seven assists. He is able to bring high production despite the opposition.

CAN YOU PLAY AGAINST AN OPPONENT?

I used to play basketball, but I'm officially retired now. In fact, I won't even touch a ball in public. But when I did play, I did all right. My son K. J. has always wanted to know at what age I did one thing or another and how well I did what I did. So, he wanted to know at what level I used to play when I was at the height of my game. In response, I told him to watch LeBron James. I said, "What he does is what I used to be able to do." I could throw a ball through my legs, pass it behind my back, throw it off the floor and dunk it, and throw it off the backboard to catch it and dunk it. Honestly, I could do all of that.

So you may be wondering why I didn't go to the NBA. The reason is that I couldn't do those things when somebody was trying to stop me. I could only do those maneuvers when I didn't have any opposition. That's what puts someone at the next level. It isn't knowing how to do things when there is no enemy around that counts, but being able to do those things when others are trying to stop us. Can we do it when someone is laughing at us and making fun of us? Can we do it when others are spreading rumors about us and posting things on Facebook? Can we do it when the other parent is acting the fool?

In Revelation 12:5, in spite of all that the enemy was throwing at her, the woman didn't let that detour her from her purpose. Even in the midst of all the harassment and all the fearsome things she saw, "She gave birth to a son, a male child, who 'will rule all the nations with an iron scepter.'" Single parents will face opposition. It may be socially, financially, spiritually, emotionally—or even a whole lot of types all at once. Don't be fooled. There will be opposition. But single parents can't let that detour them from their purpose or keep them from being productive.

GOD IS WATCHING OUT FOR US

The great news is that even when the enemy is right in front of us, God is watching over us. While the dragon was showing off his power and positioning himself right in front of the woman to reach out and devour her child as soon as he was born, the dragon was no match for the forces of God. The enemy didn't even get to touch the baby. The very second the woman gave birth to her son, "her child was snatched up to God and to his throne" (Revelation 12:5). God not only watched over the woman and her child, but He defended them as well. God went to war in defense of this woman and her baby.

We need to remember that God is fighting for us. As Yolanda Adams sings, "The battle is not yours; it's the Lord's." There is a connection between earth and heaven. Jesus once told His disciples that "whatever you bind on earth will be bound in heaven, and whatever you loose on earth will be loosed in heaven" (Matthew 18:18). The enemy is right in front of us on earth, but there are things happening in heaven that we can't even see. Just because we don't see God, however, that doesn't mean He isn't watching over us.

When we tend to doubt whether or not God is with us in this moment, we need to remember how He has been present with us in the past. There was absolutely no way that we could get that report finished on time, but it happened—because God was there. There was absolutely no way that we had money for the rent payment, but we paid it—because God was there. There was absolutely no way that we were able to remain loving and Christ-like when that person was being so mean and ugly, but we did it—because God was there. God alone makes the difference! Whether we see Him or not, God is watching over us. Whether we give Him credit or not, it's God who gets us through our battles. Whether we recognize it or not, God is watching over our children. It is God who is protecting them and helping them moment by moment and day by day.

One day as one of my sons and I were watching a playoff game on TV, during a news break we saw President Barack Obama getting off a helicopter in the middle of a field in another country. I don't remember where he was, but the camera only showed him getting off the helicopter. There was no one else around. This struck me because usually whenever we see the President getting off a plane, there is a whole entourage of people waiting for him, including all of his Secret Service agents standing nearby. But here he was, walking through the field, seemingly alone.

I said to my son, "You think he's by himself, don't you, because you don't see anyone else around? Well, if you tried to approach the President right now, you would see who all is watching over him. You would see Secret Service agents, the military, and a host of other people suddenly appear out of nowhere to protect him." Even when the President looks like he's by himself, he is not really alone. There is always someone watching over him.

Sometimes single parents feel that they are stranded all alone, trying to do everything by themselves. But that is not the case because they are never alone. We don't usually see the heavenly forces around us, but they are still there. God cares. God is watching. God will send the help that is needed when it is needed.

Just think about when this baby was born and how God snatched it away from the enemy. God will do that for our children as well. Whether married or single, a parent is not alone against the enemies that are trying to destroy his or her children. God cares. God is there. We are not alone.

If we look back over our own lives, we can all testify that God snatched us away from the enemy, too. I am not married to a wonderful woman because I have always done everything right. I am not a proud father of four great sons because I have never made a mistake. I am not the grateful pastor of an extraordinary church because I have never messed up. No, I am amazingly blessed because a loving, caring God watched over me, and before I could stray too far away from the right path, He snatched me up to Himself.

Revelation 12:5 (NLT) says, "And her child was snatched away from the dragon and was caught up to God and to his throne." I love that imagery—"caught up to God and to his throne." What a wonderful place for a child to be!

JESUS FIRST

We parents need to create an environment in our homes that will enable our children to be caught up to God. We need to have loving homes where children can feel secure and begin to understand what God's love is like. We need to pray for our children, introduce them to Jesus, and take them to church to learn about God. We should not only pray *for* our children, but pray *with* them. We need to let them hear us pray for them. We need to read the Bible with them and let them see Jesus in our daily lives—the way we talk, the way we treat others, and the values that we express by our choices.

It's good for children to play sports, learn to look their best, and become proficient in using computers. Those things are important for their mental, physical, and social well-being. But they also need to learn from an early age that it is always *Jesus first*. They need to learn how to prioritize, and they will only learn that from the way we as their parents make choices. If we stay home from church to watch a ball game, will they learn that Jesus comes first? If we spend money on fine clothes but only give what's left over to God, will they learn to make God's will their top priority? If we spend hours and hours playing video games, watching TV, or exchanging messages on Facebook, will they learn that spending time with God and family is more important than satisfying personal pleasures? Where is Jesus in our lives? If we aren't caught up to God, how can we expect that to happen for our children?

I am so thankful that my mother made us pray over our food before we ate, expected us to say our prayers before we went to bed each night, and insisted that we go to church and Sunday school. It was those habits that instilled within us a God-consciousness. The prayers before each meal—even if the meal was hamburgers cooked at home because we couldn't afford McDonald's—reminded me that there is a God and He supplies our needs. The prayers at bedtime—even though it was "Now I lay me down to sleep . . ." each night—reminded me that there is a God and that He protects and watches over me. Going to church and Sunday school—even though I would rather have been home in bed—taught me more about this God who loves me and this Jesus who died for me.

Because of our continual interaction with God as I was growing up, God was not some impersonal cosmic force, but God was *my* heavenly Father and Jesus was *my* Lord and Savior. Thanks to my mother, a single parent, I was caught up to God as a child. And now that I am no longer a child, these things are still true in my life.

BEING CAUGHT UP: DIRECTION AND DIMENSION

You may be wondering if being caught up is about "direction" or "dimension." It isn't either/or; it is both/and. To be "caught up" is the direction your child is going. Paul told the church of Thessalonica, "For the Lord himself will come down from heaven, with a loud command, with the voice of the archangel and with the trumpet call of God, and the dead in Christ will rise first. After that, we who are still alive and are left will be caught up together with them in the clouds to meet the Lord in the air. And so we will be with the Lord forever" (I Thessalonians 4:16-17). Being "caught up" in this context means that they will go in the direction of the Lord. It isn't simply being caught up into the sky or spinning in a whirlwind like in a tornado. It is being caught up "to meet the Lord in the air." That is *direction*.

In the same way, God will even now take children and move them in His direction. That is the direction of His love, His power, His authority, His guidance. So many of our children are moving in the wrong direction, but God is able to redirect them so that they are caught up and moving heaven-ward, not hell-ward. They will be moving in toward God. That is direction.

But what God wants to do is not only dealing with direction, but also with dimension. Being caught up refers to a spiritual dimension. When I was growing up and someone in church would start shouting and praising God enthusiastically in a service, we would say that person got "caught up." They had a spiritual experience in that moment that moved them to another dimension; they went to another level spiritually.

It's important to realize that two people can be in the same location and still be in different dimensions. I see that happen every Sunday in our church. Two people can leave the same house, get in the same car, come to the same church, sit on the same pew, sing the same songs, hear the same Scripture, and listen to the same sermon. Yet one of those two people is in the presence of God, while the other isn't in that same dimension.

The Lord has a spiritual dimension in mind not just for older folks in church, but also for young folks, wherever they might be. That's why your child can be in a poor school with poor teachers, yet still make it through high school and into college. Why? Because it wasn't about location. It was about the spiritual dimension in which your child lives.

The point I'm making isn't only about single-parent households either. We all know of at least one household in which both parents are present, but neither parent is present for the children in the way they should be. Two adults are in the home, but each one is doing his and her own thing. One may be on drugs while the other can't stay out of jail for any length of time.

This home situation is deplorable for their child. And yet their child meets Jesus, develops a personal relationship with the Lord, finishes high school, goes on to college and becomes a productive person in the kingdom of God and the community in which they live. Why? Because it wasn't about the home in which this child resided, but the spiritual dimension in which this child lived. In spite of this child's home environment, he or she was caught up to God and lived in a different spiritual dimension even while staying in the same physical dimension as the parents.

SPIRITUAL AIR POCKETS

If you are a parent reading this book, don't feel hopeless about where your child is right now. You may be thinking, "It's too late for my child. You don't know how lowdown my child has become. I would be too ashamed to even tell you about my child's life and behavior. I would love to see my child get caught up to God, but it's just too late for my baby." This book is in your hands today because God wants you to know that it is not too late. Look at the first part of Revelation 12:5. It says, "And her child was snatched away from the dragon." That would imply that the child was in the dragon's clutches. The dragon thought he had that child and he was going to devour it. But he couldn't. Because that is just when the child was snatched away by God and taken up to His throne. It is not too late for your child.

In July of 2013, at Indiana Dunes National Lakeshore in Michigan City, Indiana, a six-year-old boy was walking on one of the dunes known as Mount Baldy when he was swallowed up by the dune. His parents rushed over and began digging. Initially they could see him, so they dug frantically to reach him. But as they were digging, he sank farther down, until he was out of sight. As they learned later, he had fallen eleven feet under the sand. He was so far down that he was no longer even visible. The distraught parents quickly called for help. It took the authorities over three hours, but they found the boy—still alive.

You may think it was impossible that the boy could have still been alive after being buried under the sand for three hours. But there was an air pocket around him that allowed him to breathe until the crew got him out. Yes, it seemed impossible. Yes, it seemed too late to save him. But no one gave up on him. They kept working and working until they found him alive and were able to nurse him back to health.

As you look at what has happened to your own son, you may have seen him sink so low that you think it's hopeless. You may have watched your own daughter get so caught up in sin that you no longer even see her. But don't give up. You must not forget that while you are praying, God is working. You can't save your child yourself, but God can do what we cannot do.

The Scriptures speak about the breath of God. Job 33:4 says, "The Spirit of God has made me; the breath of the Almighty gives me life." John 20:22 tells us that Jesus "breathed" on His disciples and said, "Receive the Holy Spirit." Do not underestimate the breath of God. Just as God provided a pocket of air in the physical realm to help that little boy survive, so He also breathes on our children in the spiritual realm to give them life. As we pray, God breathes.

God hasn't given up on your children. He is still breathing life into them even while they are lost. God is putting a protective pocket of spiritual air around them to give them the chance to be rescued. Paul reminds us in Romans 5:8, "But God demonstrates his own love for us in this: While we were still sinners, Christ died for us." God loves us even when we are still sinners. And while we are still sinners, God sends out rescue parties to reach down and snatch us out of the clutches of the enemy. Since God doesn't give up on our children, neither should we.

GOD CARES ABOUT YOU

God cares not only about children, but also about parents. Single parent, God cares about you. In Revelation 12:6 (NLT), we read, "And the woman fled into the wilderness, where God had prepared a place to care for her for 1,260 days." It doesn't say, "God hurried to make a place for the woman." It doesn't say, "When God saw what was happening, God realized He needed to find a place for the woman." No, it says that "God had prepared a place to care for her."

This place was prepared for her even before she got pregnant. God knows not only the past and the present, but also the future. God knew one day she would need a place, so He already had that place lovingly prepared for her. It was a place where she would be cared for—fed, clothed, nourished, and protected.

170

There are times when single parents feel so alone. A single mother has to announce her pregnancy to a lot of people who don't understand and are sometimes critical and judgmental. Instead of her parents embracing her, they put her out of the house. Instead of the teacher working with her to help her finish that year of school, the teacher gives her a look that calls her a name even without opening his mouth. Instead of an employer understanding the pressures young people face, the employer makes her job so impossible that she has to quit.

Even if others are kind and understanding, there is still a loneliness that only a single mother can feel. She sees her pregnant married friend and how much that woman's husband loves her and cares for her, and the single mom feels very much alone. She watches a movie in which the pregnant woman and her husband go for an ultrasound and share a loving embrace after seeing their baby for the first time, and the single mom feels very much alone. She thinks about the future and all of the expenses and challenges of bringing up a child, and the single mom feels very much alone.

When she goes into labor and suffers the pain of childbirth, when she has to leave that little baby in someone else's hands in order to work to feed that child, when she has to rush that child to the hospital by herself when the little one is injured, when her child cries because he has no father to take to school on the day dads are visiting, when she can't afford to do all the special things that other parents do for their children, when she goes by herself to talk to the principal after her child gets in trouble at school, the single mom feels very much alone—over and over again. Except for the pregnancy and birth, this is often just as true for single dads who are trying to care for their children by themselves.

During those difficult times, single parents may be tempted to actually believe that they are all alone. But that is not true. God is there. The God who knew she would one day get pregnant, the God who knew he would one day be raising a baby alone, is there. What's more, God has prepared a place for the single parent. He knows what a single parent is going through. He understands the pain, the loneliness, and the stress that is a continual part of life. So

God, in His loving kindness and tender mercies, has already prepared a place. This is a place of nourishment and restoration.

Single parent, God knows that you are in a battle. From the moment you conceive, you are in a battle for your child. You fight to do the right things; you fight to provide for your child; you fight to bring your child up to know the Lord; and you find that you are in a continual battle over the life of your child. But that battle is worth it. The child to whom you gave birth is worth battling for.

Sometimes when things get especially rough, a single parent may begin to wonder if it really is worth it. Is it really worth the constant battles? Is it worth the continual struggle? I am so thankful that my mother never gave up on me. I know there were times that she felt like throwing in the towel, but she didn't. I am the youngest of four children, and just as each one of the others went through a season in which they acted crazy and caused her grief, I did that too. But she never gave up on me. Even when I couldn't see it myself, she knew I was worth battling for. No matter what you are going through right now, it is worth the battle. And you are not fighting alone.

PREPARED FOR THE PLACE PREPARED FOR US

We've read about how God had prepared a place for this woman, and God has prepared a place for us. But sometimes, we are not prepared for the place that is prepared for us. We may want to go into a friendship that is prepared for us, but we don't know how to be a good friend. We may want to enter into a positive, healthy relationship, but we are dysfunctional ourselves. We may want to get married and live happily ever after, but we aren't even happy with ourselves. How can we expect someone else to like us and be happy with us if we can't stand to be alone with ourselves? We have to be ready for the things God has ready for us.

So how do we prepare? In Revelation 12:1, it says the woman was "clothed with the sun." Now, however we want to interpret that symbolically and theologically, being clothed with the sun would indicate that the woman was enlightened. It was obvious from what she was wearing that this was not a woman operating in darkness.

That verse also says that she had "the moon under her feet." The moon doesn't produce its own light. The moon reflects the light from the sun. The woman could operate in the light because she was in a place that she reflected the light from the sun. Her stand and the way she walked reflected the sun.

Finally, the woman had "a crown of twelve stars on her head." Whether symbolically the stars stand for the twelve tribes of Israel, the twelve apostles, or whatever, it would indicate that her mind is enlightened. The stars in her crown shine. There is a light on her head that illuminates her thinking. This woman is prepared by what she was wearing on her body, where her feet were standing, and what she had on her head.

She was also prepared in that she was pregnant. Remember that this woman represented Mary and her baby symbolized Jesus. Jesus came about because the Holy Spirit overshadowed Mary. She became pregnant because she was in the presence of God. Similarly, when we spend time alone with God and become intimate with Him, He will fill us with Jesus.

KEEP IN STEP WITH THE SEASON

Not only was this a prepared woman going to a prepared place, but she also went at a rapid pace. Revelation 12:6 says the woman "fled" to the prepared place. She wasn't someone who put God off until the next week, next month, or next year. She immediately ran from the place where she was and fled to the place God wanted her to be.

If we aren't in the place God has prepared for us, that means we are out of place, misplaced, and displaced. What we walk away from can determine what we walk into. If we are not willing to leave where we are displaced, we will never get to the place we belong. We have to *run* to get to the place God has prepared for us.

When we start to leave the place we are, we can count on hearing negative things from others. When we try to leave an unhealthy, dysfunctional relationship, that person will tell us that we'll never make it alone. That person will tell us that no one else will want us and we aren't any good anyhow. But we have to listen to the One who has a place prepared for us. When He says it's time to go, we should run and not walk from wherever we are to the place where He is leading.

Sometimes we are in a hurry about everything except the things of God. We are in a hurry to get into a relationship, in a hurry to go to a club, in a hurry to socialize, in a hurry to get rich, in a hurry to have some fun, and in a hurry to go somewhere that ultimately has nothing for us. We run into a relationship, only to find there is no love there. We run to a club for a good time, only to end up feeling guilty. We run to socialize, but end up feeling alone in a crowd. We run to get money, only to find that money doesn't satisfy what we really need. We run to have fun, but go back home feeling empty inside. All these other "places" cannot satisfy like the place God has prepared for us.

It is true that in different seasons of life, we move at different paces. Psalm 23:4 says, "Even though I walk through the darkest valley . . ." There are times we have to walk. First of all, when we are going through a dark valley, we need to walk, not run, because we cannot see what's ahead of us. If we run in the dark, we are likely to stumble or even to fall off a cliff because we cannot see in the dark. The dark times are also those periods in our life when we can often hear God better. We know we can't find our way ourselves, so we listen to God and let Him speak to us. We find ourselves obeying God because we recognize how vulnerable we are without Him. When we come out on the other side of the darkest valley, we will have learned from God. We will know how to handle our anointing, how to handle our relationships, how to handle our finances, and how to handle even our enemies. So we *walk* through the dark valleys.

But there are other times that we have to get in a hurry and run. Second Timothy 2:22 says, "Flee the evil desires of youth," or, as it says in *The Living Bible*, "Run from anything that gives you the evil thoughts that young men often have." Run from sexual immorality. Run from relationships that will drag you down. Run from so-called friends who want to get you drunk or high. Run from anything and anyone who would take you away from your intimacy with God. As country music artist Kenny Rogers sings, "You've got to know when to walk away, know when to run."

He Prepared for Us the Church

But keep in mind we aren't just running *from* something; we are also running *to* the very place that God has prepared for us. In this place, God will have people who can nurture us, refresh us, and care for us. How long will that last? For the woman of Revelation 12, the Bible says 1,260 days, which is three-and-a-half years. When I read that, my question to God was, "If you have prepared this place for us and we have gone through so much to get there, why is it only going to last 1,260 days? Why not longer?"

In response, God reminded me that this revelation of John takes place in the last days. This is only midway in the seven-year period of the Great Tribulation. There are only 1,260 days left before the Great Tribulation would be over. God is saying, "I'm going to see you through to the end." This means that there is only a limited number of days that the enemy is allowed to harass us. We don't have to jump off a bridge, put a bullet through our heads, or slit our wrists. We don't have to give up. Whatever trials and tribulations we are going through right now are limited. God won't let the devil keep at us and at us until he finally wears us down. No, we need to stay strong only until God says, "Enough!" Then he has to leave us alone. Grandma and those in her day used to say, "I'm so glad that trouble don't last always." They knew that the devil's days were numbered.

In reading about this prepared place, I also asked God, "Where is this place?" At first, I thought it was in heaven. But God showed me that Revelation 12:6 says that the woman fled into the wilderness. There is no wilderness in heaven. This place that God has prepared for each of us is right here on earth. But where is such a place? Where will people nurture us, help us, heal us, renew us, and refresh us?

That place God has prepared for us is the church that Jesus has established. When I think of all that I have gone through personally—the physical, emotional, mental, and social attacks—I am so thankful that I could run to the house of God and find help, healing, nurturing, and renewal. In this world we have tribulation, but in the church we have triumph. In the world we have crisis after crisis, but in the church we have care and comfort. In the world we have confusion, but in the church we have peace. We may feel down when we're out in the world, but we feel lifted up when we come to the house of God.

No, the church isn't yet perfect. The church is composed of people just like you and me. And no matter how much we wish we were perfect, we aren't. First John 1:10 (NLT) says, "If we claim we have not sinned, we are calling God a liar and showing that his word has no place in our hearts." So, as we become part of the church, we should strive to give to others what we ourselves need so desperately. We who need forgiveness for ourselves should be willing to forgive others. We who need to be restored should be willing to restore others. We who need grace should be willing to be gracious to others. We who need love should be willing to love others. We who need Jesus should be willing to show Jesus to others. The last part of Matthew 10:8 says, "Freely you have received; freely give." The church is a place where we receive freely and give freely so that no one lacks anything.

The church is the place God has prepared for us. It is there that we will be nurtured, healed, restored, and set free. Christ is the Head of the church. It is in Him that all of these things reside. In Him there is healing; in Him there is power; in Him there is hope; in Him there is peace; in Him there is salvation; in Him there is joy; in Him there is freedom; in Him there is love. And when He lives in us, those things can be found in us as well. In the church, there are people who have been healed, so they want others to be well. There are people who have been revived, so they want others to be recharged. There are people who have been brought back to life, so they want others to live again. There are people who have been loved into the kingdom, so they want to lovingly invite others in as well.

We must not miss the place God has prepared for us—the place where we will be cared for.

Dear God,

We thank You for loving our children and loving us as well. Thank You for the hope that it is never too late—not for our children and not for us. For our children, we pray that they will love You and desire to serve You above all others. For us, we pray that we may be fully prepared to enter the place You have prepared for us, the place of our destiny. God, the battle has been long and hard, but we thank You for keeping us and thank You loving us. We trust You now to continue to work in our hearts and work in the hearts of our children. Keep us true to You in these last days and let our lights shine out to draw others to You. Work in us and in the church to make Your people all that You want us to be. Amen.